"Every illustration from the brilliant, soulful Haley Weaver is like a big scoop of peanut butter ice cream: the kind of satisfaction you never knew you needed. She speaks directly to your inner child but with a perspective that's necessary for adulting. This book is a must-read for anyone who struggles with their internal voice versus their outside persona, which is a struggle we probably all thought was 'just us' until Haley normalized it! Thank you, Haley, for your compassion, and for seeing us as beautiful—just like your drawings are. What a perfect gift for anyone who's embarking on a new adventure, whether tiny or enormous."

—Mari Andrew, *New York Times* bestselling author
of *Am I There Yet?* and *My Inner Sky*

"Haley Weaver deftly uses the comics format to present a range of characters as simple shapes—herself, other people, and a chatty range of coping mechanisms—allowing her to present heavy material with sweetness and humor. The Anxiety character, an insightful, nervous little black cloud, fights to be heard, and ultimately, the author learns how to live with—and even appreciate—his persistence."

—Ellen Forney, *New York Times* bestselling author of *Marbles*

"*Give Me Space but Don't Go Far* is as vulnerable as it is adorable, and deceptively cute for all its poeticism and profundity. Perfect for any recent graduate or young person struggling with anxiety, this book will teach you how to shine a warm light on the parts of yourself you most want to obscure in darkness."

—Erin Williams, author of *Commute* and coauthor
of *The Big Activity Book for Anxious People*

"This book gives me all the feels! Like all of them: *Give Me Space but Don't Go Far* is hilarious, tender, smart, honest, painful, poignant, illuminating, and totally made me cry at the end. Haley Weaver has done what I thought was impossible: tell a deeply personal story of her relationship with anxiety through a fully realized and delightfully illustrated cast of coping-mechanism characters, each of whom personifies the sneaky ways our brains work for and against us. In doing so, Weaver educates and empowers readers to see their own anxiety as a relationship to be tended and managed with support, not feared. The clean and dynamic drawing style—with bodies shaped as hearts, scribble-blobs, and sunglasses-wearing rectangles—and hilarious speech bubbles and asides are a huge part of this wonderful book's disarming charm."

—Kelcey Ervick, author of *The Keeper*

"What a relatable, honest, and engaging body of work. This book is a cozy and colorful reminder to be patient with ourselves and redefine anxiety's role in our own stories."

—Danielle Coke Balfour, creator of Oh Happy Dani
and author of *A Heart on Fire*

"A heartwarming and empowering reminder of the wisdom and care that's nested within our (sometimes scary and overwhelming) scribbly anxieties."

—Ariella Elovic, author of *Cheeky*

"Sweet, profound, funny, and unwaveringly honest, this debut by Haley Weaver made me gasp with recognition, laugh with delight, and rethink how I relate to my own emotions. Haley has a knack for capturing the nuances and personality of her anxiety. And while no two people's experiences are alike, I found myself relating to this book at every turn. A must-read for anyone navigating their mental health and hoping to understand themselves better."

—Olivia de Recat, author of *Drawn Together*

# GIVE ME SPACE BUT DON'T GO FAR

## MY UNLIKELY FRIENDSHIP WITH ANXIETY

### HALEY WEAVER

AVERY | AN IMPRINT OF PENGUIN RANDOM HOUSE | NEW YORK

AVERY

an imprint of Penguin Random House LLC
penguinrandomhouse.com

Most Avery books are available at special quantity discounts for bulk
purchase for sales promotions, premiums, fundraising, and educational
needs. Special books or book excerpts also can be created to fit specific
needs. For details, write SpecialMarkets@penguinrandomhouse.com.

LIBRARY OF CONGRESS CATALOGING-IN-PUBLICATION DATA
has been applied for.

ISBN 9780593539330 (trade paperback)
ISBN 9780593539347 (ebook)

Printed in China

1 3 5 7 9 10 8 6 4 2

Book design by Lorie Pagnozzi

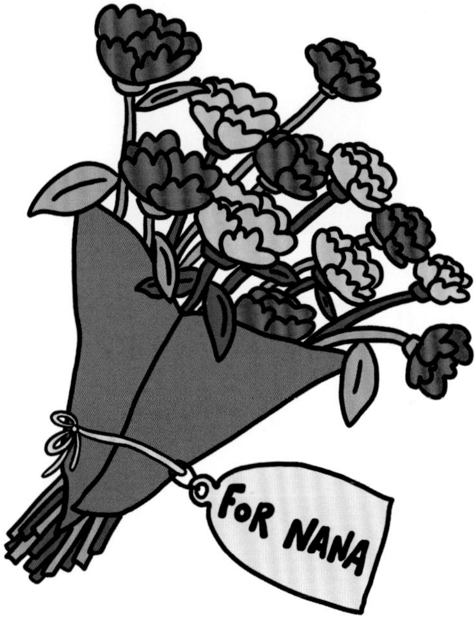
FOR NANA

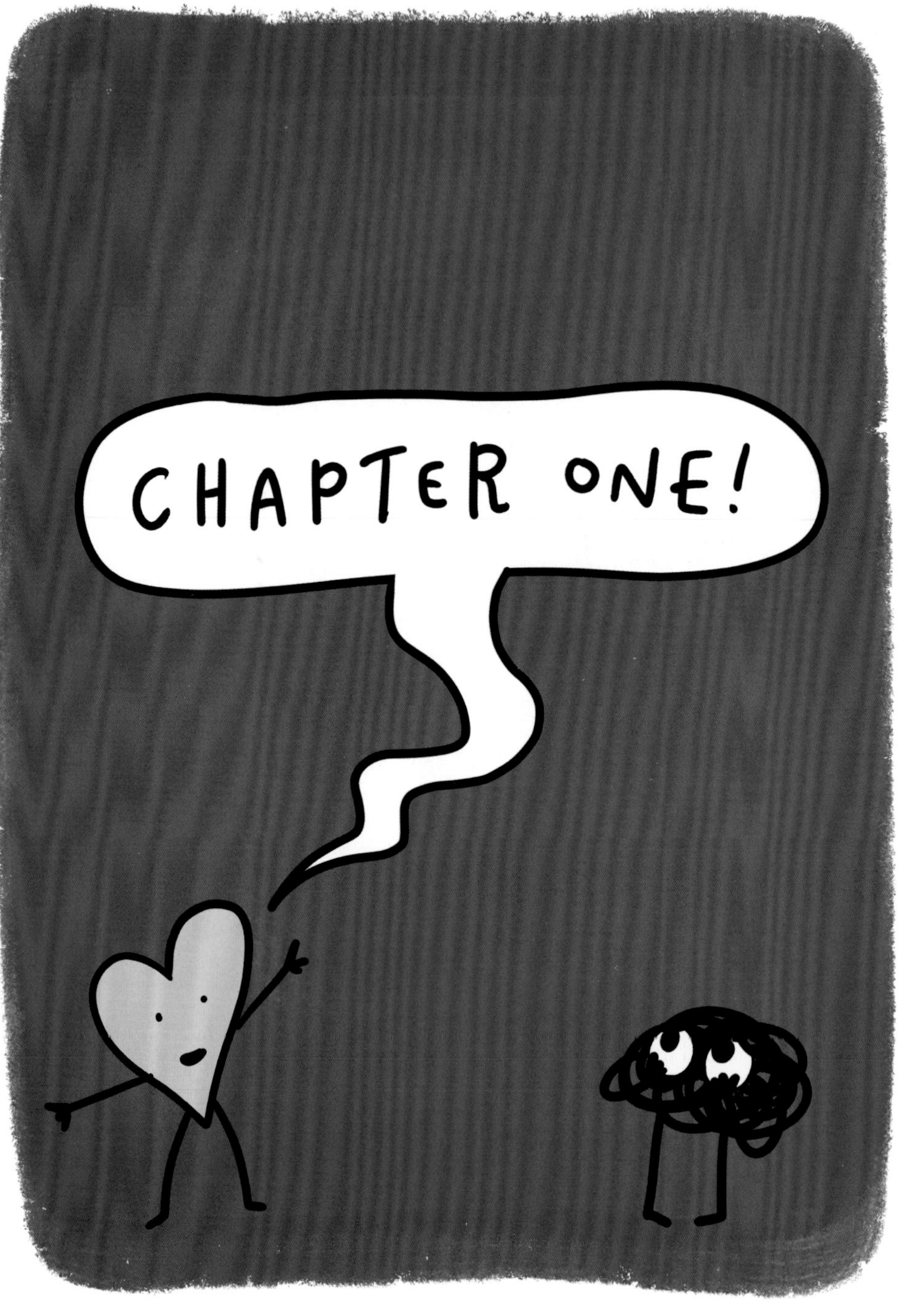
CHAPTER ONE!

It was way past my bedtime on the night I first discovered the monster under my bed.

Okay, "monster" might have been a stretch. All I could actually see was a shadow looming across my bedroom wall like a heavy rain cloud.

I waited for something terrible to happen—a growl in my ear, a clawed hand around my ankle, a declaration that four-year-old girls were on the menu tonight—but if anything, the shadow just shifted every once in a while, a reminder that it was there.

When I woke up the next morning, I wondered if I'd made the whole thing up, but the shadow returned the next night, and the night after that. At first, I pretended my mind was just playing a cruel trick on me.

But then it began to talk.

The voice was quiet and shaky, but it commanded the whole room.

Night after night, I hoped I'd be able to fall asleep without hearing the voice. But night after night, it drifted up from beneath the bed like a foul odor, too distracting to ignore.

It got even scarier when I began to sense its presence during the daytime.

Years later, in the office of my elementary school counselor, I'd learn that this creature had a name.

Even if Anxiety wasn't a monster, I had no interest in keeping him in my life.

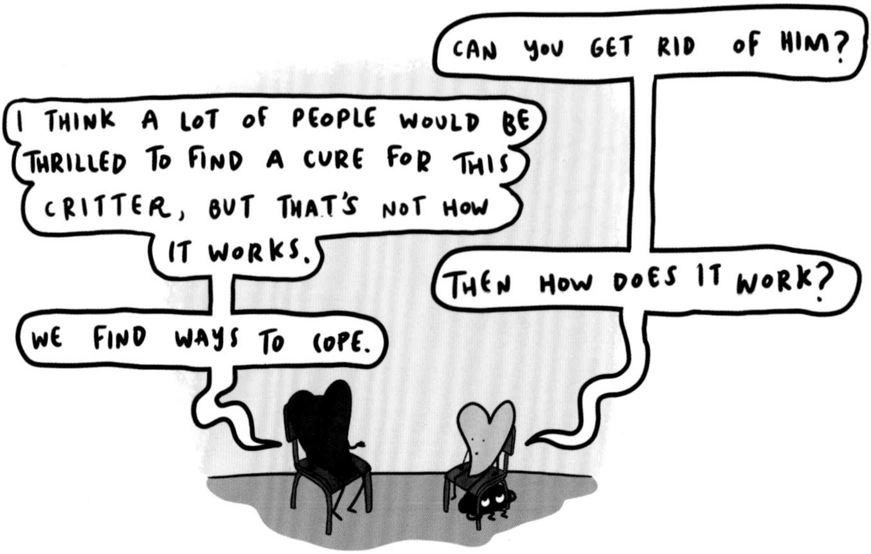
CAN YOU GET RID OF HIM?
I THINK A LOT OF PEOPLE WOULD BE THRILLED TO FIND A CURE FOR THIS CRITTER, BUT THAT'S NOT HOW IT WORKS.
THEN HOW DOES IT WORK?
WE FIND WAYS TO COPE.

Coping. I could try that.

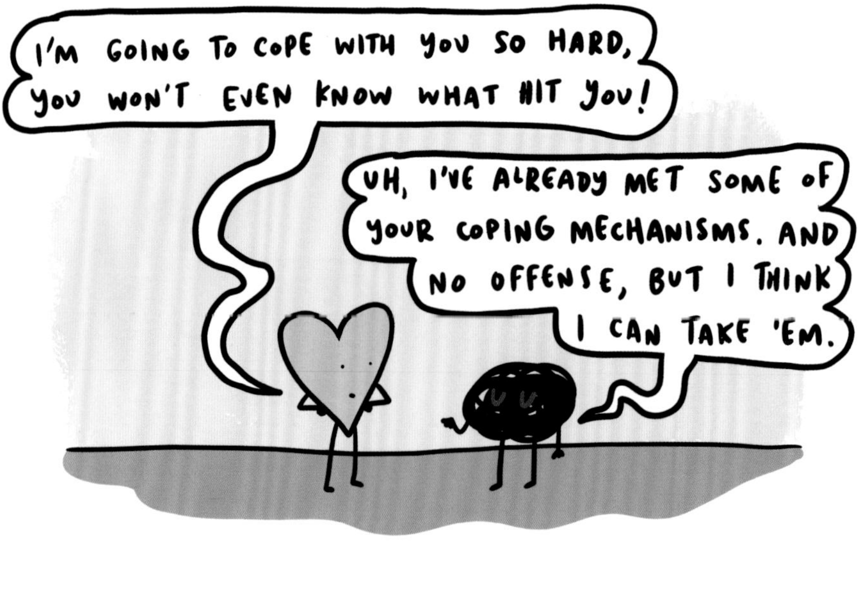
I'M GOING TO COPE WITH YOU SO HARD, YOU WON'T EVEN KNOW WHAT HIT YOU!
UH, I'VE ALREADY MET SOME OF YOUR COPING MECHANISMS. AND NO OFFENSE, BUT I THINK I CAN TAKE 'EM.

It took me a moment to figure out who he was talking about.

There was the Hurricane, who believed nothing exhausted Anxiety quite like a tantrum.

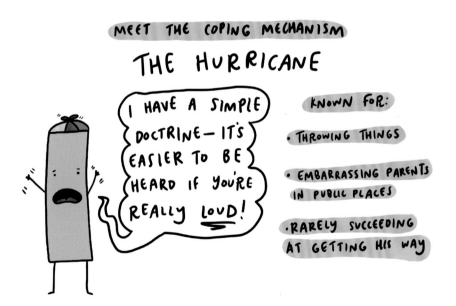

The Hurricane likened an outburst to the perfect storm: dark sky, howling winds, absolute downpour. In theory, it always sounded like a great way to get Anxiety's voice out of my head.

In practice, not so much.

And on the opposite side of the volume dial was the Hider, who did not like to be seen at all.

Whenever Anxiety worried about how I was being perceived, the Hider strategized ways to achieve maximum coverage with minimal contact.

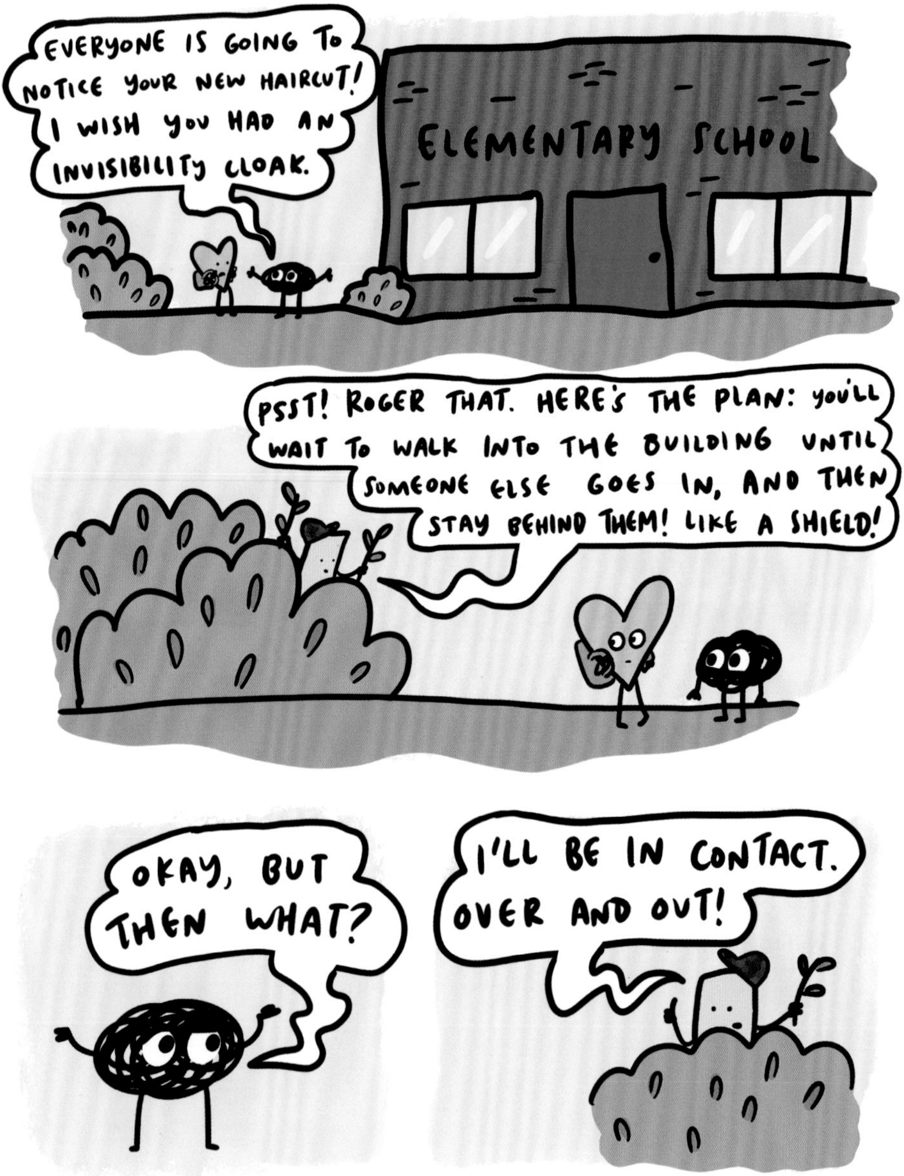
EVERYONE IS GOING TO NOTICE YOUR NEW HAIRCUT! I WISH YOU HAD AN INVISIBILITY CLOAK.
ELEMENTARY SCHOOL
PSST! ROGER THAT. HERE'S THE PLAN: YOU'LL WAIT TO WALK INTO THE BUILDING UNTIL SOMEONE ELSE GOES IN, AND THEN STAY BEHIND THEM! LIKE A SHIELD!
OKAY, BUT THEN WHAT?
I'LL BE IN CONTACT. OVER AND OUT!

But out of all my early coping mechanisms, the Vault had the biggest choke hold on me.

She showed up as a mode of protection, helping me avoid slipping into too vulnerable a space by diverting even the most direct questions to something else.

These were just the first of many coping mechanisms. More would show up as I grew, organizing themselves before me like toy soldiers. For a while, I fully expected them to protect me at all costs—or at least keep Anxiety out of my immediate space.

This feat would be harder than expected. Not unlike a houseguest overstaying their welcome, Anxiety seemed to lack any awareness that his presence bothered me.

Surely the more coping mechanisms I had, the easier it would be to kick him off the couch for good. Right?

Wrong. It would take me years to realize Anxiety wasn't squatting rent-free in my brain, but rather living there as a permanent, imperfect roommate. His name was on the lease, like it or not.

This is the story of how I realized I wasn't ever going to untangle myself from him, not entirely.

This is the story of learning to live with the tangle and depend on my coping mechanisms for support.

This is the story of hearing Anxiety speak, but not knowing how to listen.

This is the story of slowly learning how to speak back.

# EVERYONE'S ANXIETY LOOKS A LITTLE DIFFERENT.

SOMEONE'S ANXIETY

SOMEONE'S ANXIETY

SOMEONE'S ANXIETY

SOMEONE'S ANXIETY

SOMEONE'S ANXIETY

# THIS STORY IS ABOUT MINE

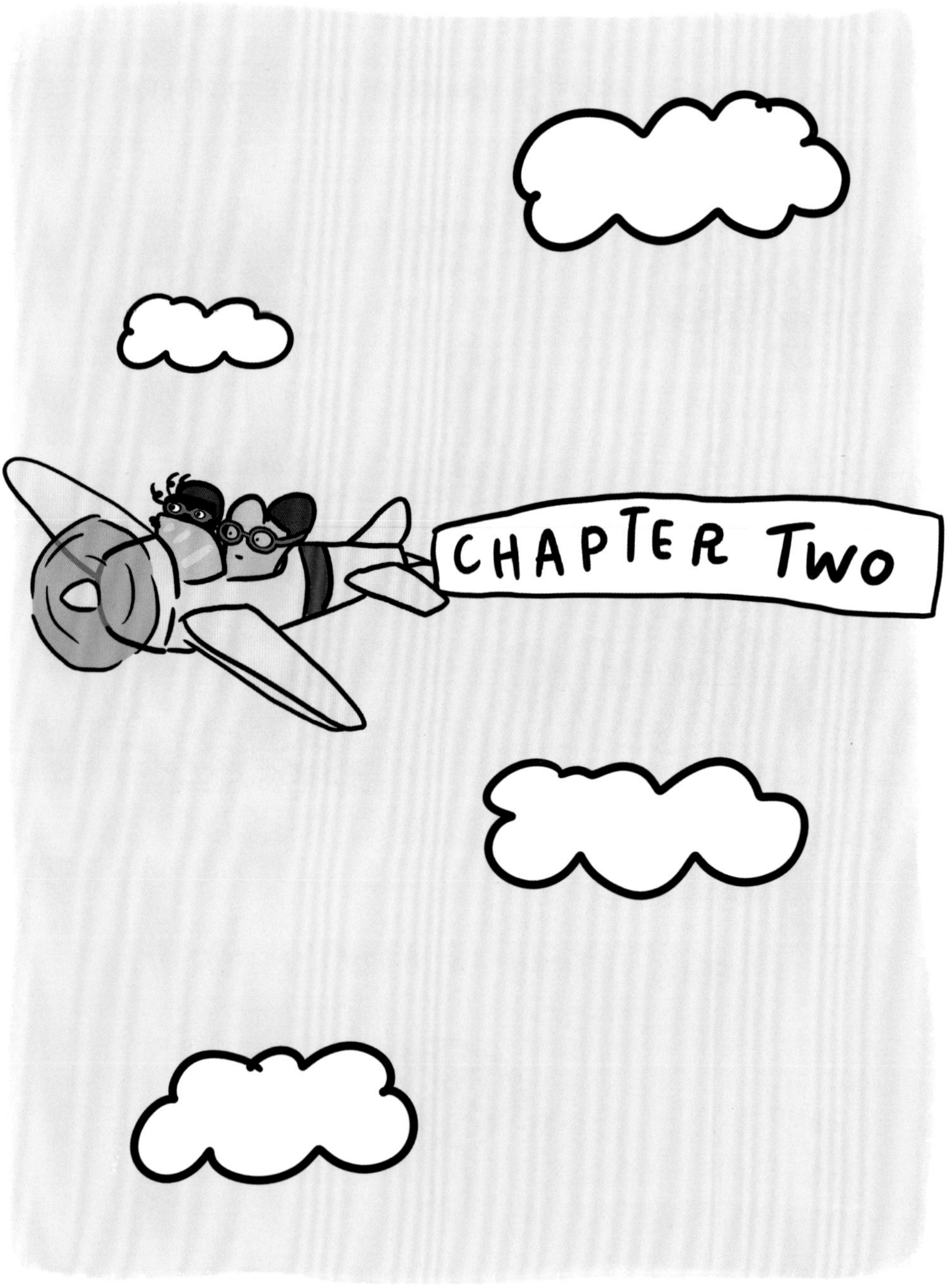
CHAPTER TWO

They say nothing good happens after 2 a.m., and I was finding that to be the truth from a motel bed in Middle of Nowhere, USA.

No, this wasn't a Tinder date gone awry, nor was it the set for a horror film. Instead, the dim glow of my phone reflected in my bloodshot eyes and my thumb was like an automatic lever as I scrolled.

It felt like a horror movie, though. I kept thinking about my alarm, set to ring in just five hours. And more terrifying than anything else was the disturbing realization that I didn't feel in control. Someone else was.

But I'm getting ahead of myself.

Instead let's begin five days earlier in my parents' driveway—two months after my twenty-fourth birthday, one month after I quit my first desk job, and two weeks before I'd officially live in Seattle, Washington. Two weeks, because that's how long it would take to drive there from my hometown in North Carolina. And today, that drive would begin.

My mom, a planning aficionado, had plotted a route that hit cities, national parks, and ghost towns with equal fervor. She graciously took time off to help me make the move, while my dad planned to fly out a week in and help us through the final stretch.

*Why Seattle?* This was the question my co-workers and friends asked when I announced my impending departure, and I never knew quite what to say. There wasn't a new job waiting for me, and the only person I would know out there was my college roommate Sam, who had convinced me to join her as she made her own Pacific Northwestern move.

But the real answer was that there wasn't a good answer at all. Perhaps it was a little bit of everything: life felt stale lately, I wanted to escape my problems, I missed living with Sam, and—most shamefully of all—what if there was a better version of my life out there? I clung to that possibility as we pulled out of the driveway, my eyes trained on my dad waving from the sidewalk.

The first few hours disappeared as quickly as they came. Mom had me pull up directions to our first stop, Nashville, while we traded off picking songs and ate gummy bears by the handful. The sky was as blue as I'd ever seen it, stretched out before us like a blank slate. Things felt good, but Anxiety was a little agitated.

We'd barely parked when I hurried out of the car and into the rest stop, making a point not to invite Anxiety along.

I looked to my right, shocked at who I saw applying lipstick in the mirror just two sinks down.

## MEET THE COPING MECHANISM
# THE DISTRACTOR

KNOWN FOR:

- MAKING IMPULSIVE DECISIONS

- FINDING THE STRANGEST INTERNET RABBIT HOLES

- PROCRASTINATING ON THE PROJECT DUE TOMORROW

*I WATCHED HOURS OF MAKEUP TUTORIALS ON YOUTUBE TO ACHIEVE THIS LOOK.*

The Distractor had a talent for showing up when I wanted to avoid my feelings, and she was funnier and louder and cooler than anyone else I knew.

Anxiety was less of a fan.

To be fair, the Distractor had no interest in hanging out with Anxiety either.

Back in the car, the Distractor took up what little space was left in the back seat, edging Anxiety farther away from me as she made herself comfortable.

For the uninitiated, the wheel of distractions was a massive roulette-style wheel mechanism, each of its dazzling wedges obnoxiously bright and labeled with a method of diversion. But in this game, there were no cash prizes or tropical vacations up for grabs. Instead, the reward was a form of distraction, be it procrastination or disassociation or simply a detour from reality.

WHEEL OF DISTRACTIONS, AGE 8

The options on the wheel changed as I grew, flashing with new ways to draw me farther from facing Anxiety head-on.

WHEEL OF DISTRACTIONS, AGE 15

And the one the Distractor brought today did not disappoint.

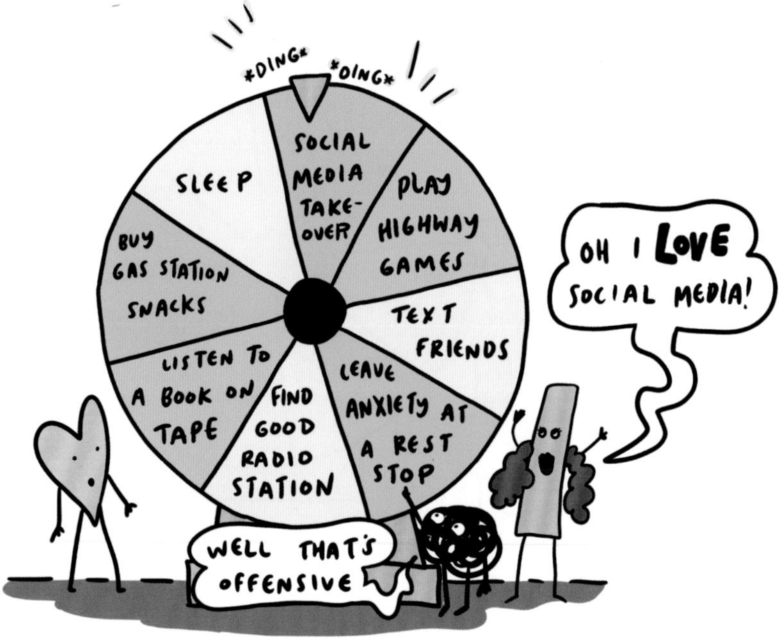
*DING* *DING*
SOCIAL MEDIA TAKE-OVER
PLAY HIGHWAY GAMES
TEXT FRIENDS
LEAVE ANXIETY AT A REST STOP
FIND GOOD RADIO STATION
LISTEN TO A BOOK ON TAPE
BUY GAS STATION SNACKS
SLEEP
OH I LOVE SOCIAL MEDIA!
WELL THAT'S OFFENSIVE

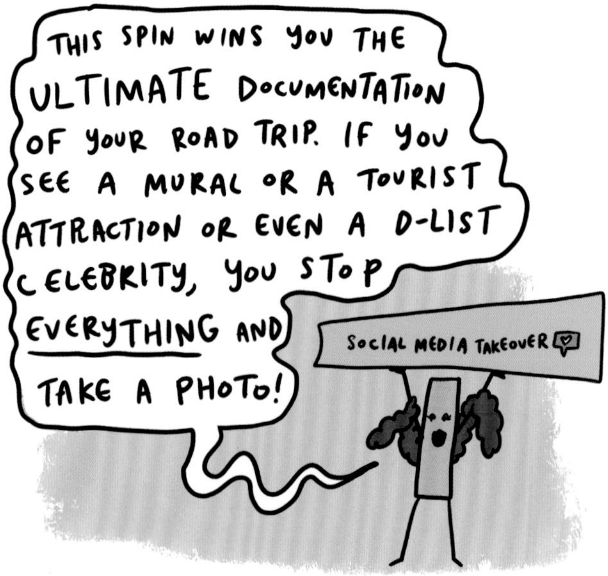
THIS SPIN WINS YOU THE ULTIMATE DOCUMENTATION OF YOUR ROAD TRIP. IF YOU SEE A MURAL OR A TOURIST ATTRACTION OR EVEN A D-LIST CELEBRITY, YOU STOP EVERYTHING AND TAKE A PHOTO!
SOCIAL MEDIA TAKEOVER

The Distractor wasn't sure exactly how we'd make a lot of internet-ready content from the car, but then Mom interrupted.

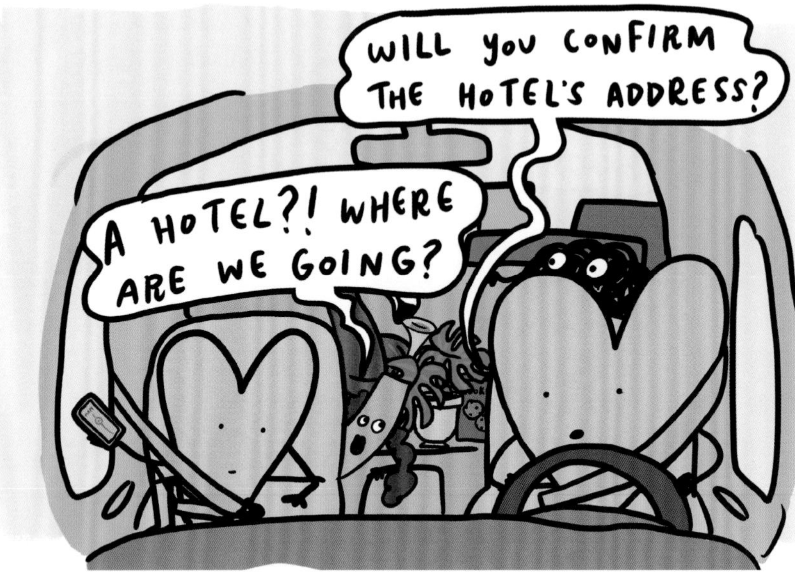
WILL YOU CONFIRM THE HOTEL'S ADDRESS?
A HOTEL?! WHERE ARE WE GOING?

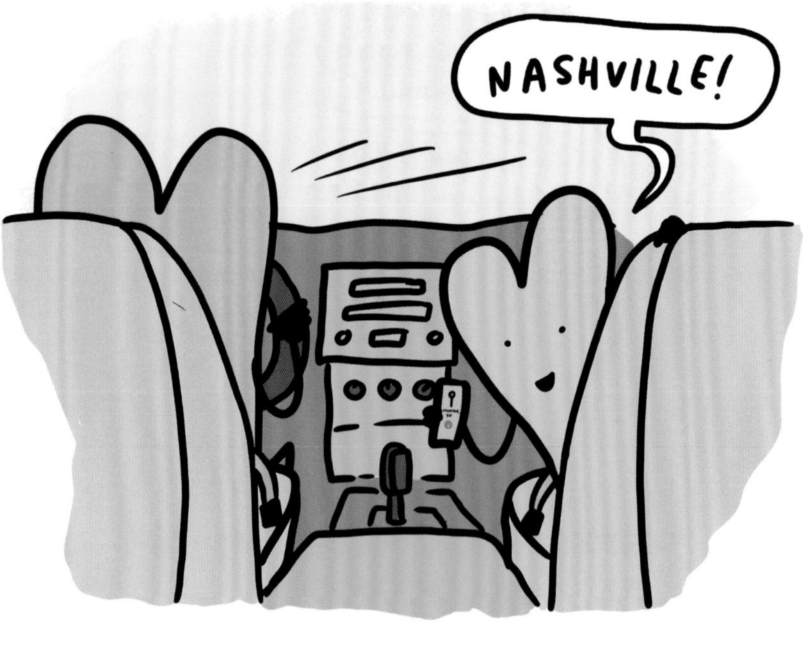
NASHVILLE!

And so it was settled: the trip officially became a highlight reel, and Nashville was the perfect place to start. As we drove through the city, the Distractor mapped out buildings adorned in bright paint and restaurants with aesthetic dishes and rooftops with unparalleled views. And later that night, the Distractor cheered when my mom found a free concert on the lawn near our hotel.

It didn't take long to flood my social media channels with filtered moments—a selfie with Mom as we slurped ramen, a shot of me looking up at a sculpture, a video of the sunset as we drove through Saint Louis. Whenever Anxiety tried to creep into the background, the Distractor did her best to keep him out of frame.

I couldn't help thinking this was one of the Distractor's best anxiety interferences yet: when one post stopped getting engagement, I'd quickly share something else, ready to bask in the glow of likes and comments and the occasional direct message.

As we drove on through the end of the first week, my camera roll only grew.

It was somewhere along a particularly grueling expanse of flat midwestern highway that things started to slow down.

Mom and I found a motel on a random highway exit that night, where our room smelled like mothballs and the cell signal was too weak to properly load anything more than an incoming text message.

But for the first time on the trip, there wasn't much to choose from.

That left Anxiety and me alone for the first time in a while.

But even as I said it, my voice sounded meek, like all my fears were overtaking the happy online facade I'd put on.

And with that, Anxiety rolled away, leaving me blinking into the darkness as his words echoed in my head. I couldn't fall asleep, not until after the Distractor stumbled back into the room an hour later.

And even though it was 2 a.m., the hour of bad decisions, I was just relieved to be thinking of anything else.

I felt like shit the next day.

I slumped down and pressed my sunglasses closer to my face, ignoring both the Distractor and the sun shining through the windshield. I snuck a peek up to the rearview mirror, hoping to catch Anxiety's eye, but he stared out the window, his vision trained on the grassy median slicing the highway in two.

But I pretended I couldn't hear her and shut my eyes instead.

It was somewhere in South Dakota that we saw the first billboard for the Corn Palace, a burst of yellow among exit signs and telephone wires.

It was early, so the parking lot was only dotted with cars. Mom found a prime parking spot in front of a plastic cornstalk sculpture with a cartoonish face peering out from the husk.

The Corn Palace itself was interstate royalty, with grand castle turrets and onion domes and triangular flags fluttering in the wind. But what really captured my attention were the long wooden frames along the sides of the building, filled with cobs cut lengthwise and nailed into place. The corn, all different colors, made up stunning murals, or as the Corn Palace called them on a placard, "crop art."

But inside was different. No longer shadowed by the dazzling exterior of the kingdom, we walked under the fluorescent lights in the lobby and into an auditorium, where we were the only people besides a man driving a floor scrubber across the stage. The chairs were folded up, and when we spoke, our voices echoed throughout the space.

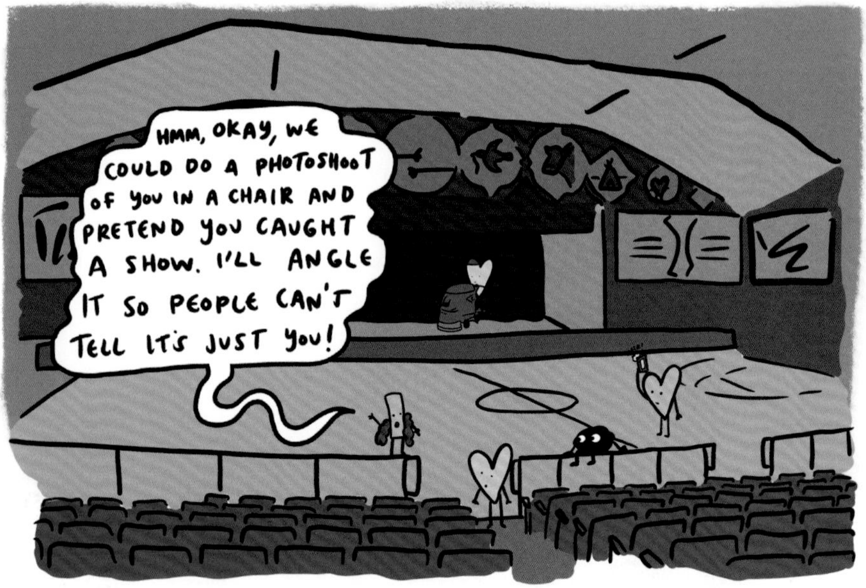
HMM, OKAY, WE COULD DO A PHOTOSHOOT OF YOU IN A CHAIR AND PRETEND YOU CAUGHT A SHOW. I'LL ANGLE IT SO PEOPLE CAN'T TELL IT'S JUST YOU!

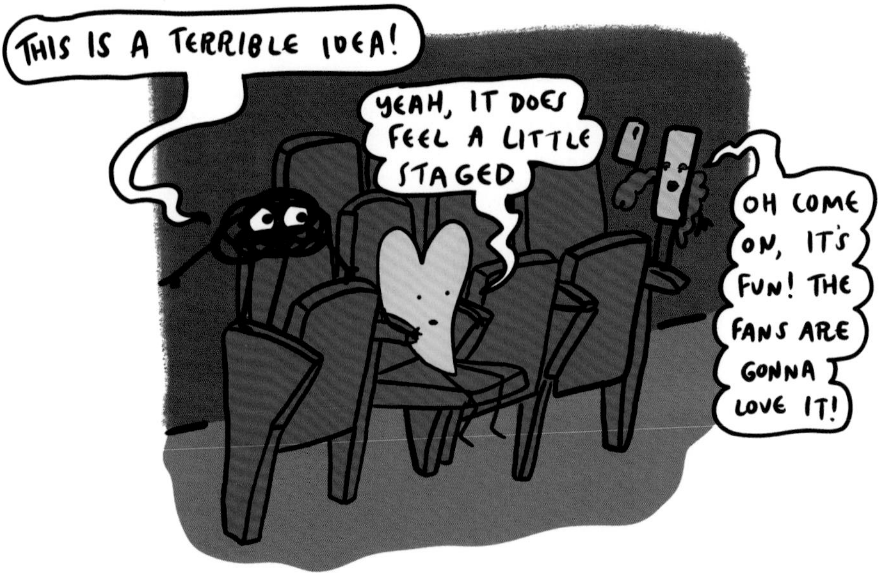
THIS IS A TERRIBLE IDEA!
YEAH, IT DOES FEEL A LITTLE STAGED
OH COME ON, IT'S FUN! THE FANS ARE GONNA LOVE IT!

But I wasn't having fun. It felt as if I was building my own roadside attraction online, one where the outside was enticing and beautiful and worth pausing to look at, while inside I was starting to feel as hollow as the empty auditorium I sat in.

Anxiety found me on a bench near the entrance.

I had to admit that Anxiety had a point. Even next to this eccentric building in a state I'd never stepped foot in before today, I wasn't able to fully appreciate it. My mind was tugging me elsewhere, to the fears I'd been pushing down about uprooting my life and starting over.

I kept thinking about what Anxiety had said as we drove the four hours to the Rapid City Regional Airport, where my dad had flown to meet us on the last leg of the trip.

Much to the Distractor's delight, I opted for the first shift of sitting in the back seat.

As the Distractor scrolled through a mood board she'd put together of people posed on mountaintops and by rivers and even under a spattering of stars, I tried to muster up excitement, but I could feel Anxiety's eyes on me, patiently waiting for my attention. And that's kind of how the long drive to Cody, Wyoming, felt: Anxiety and the Distractor were playing a game of tug-of-war, and I was the rope in between them.

By the time we dropped our luggage in the motel that evening, I felt stretched thin.

The Distractor was waving at me, spinning the wheel of distractions at an unsettling speed.

But my distraction fatigue had officially transitioned to distraction exhaustion, so I leaned into my mom and cried some more.

I woke up the next morning just feet away from where my parents still slept. Part of me felt embarrassed for breaking down, but another part of me felt relieved, like I'd finally taken off a too-tight pair of shoes after a long day. We had just under a week left until we hit Seattle, and it suddenly felt clear that I couldn't control what would come once I got there, and maybe that was okay. I looked over at Anxiety and the Distractor, relieved to see them both snoring on a pillow.

There's not really a happy ending, or an ending at all, really. Instead, the drive, and life, continued. We drove through Yellowstone and stopped at the Grand Prismatic Spring, where, much to the Distractor's delight, we took dozens of photos.

We ate dinner in the Grand Tetons, with a view of the jagged mountain range stark against the sunset. Anxiety saddled up to the table as I talked more about the things I was worried about.

We even spent a night in a bed-and-breakfast in Bozeman, where my parents and I were convinced the woman at the front desk was a ghost.

Late the next afternoon, we finally started seeing exit signs for Seattle.

The sky was overcast as we drove through downtown, the tall gray buildings as muted as the clouds behind them.

Mom parked near the market at a small grassy park that overlooked the Puget Sound. We got out of the car, our legs tingling after being still for so long, and we walked toward the water, the wind greeting us in gusts.

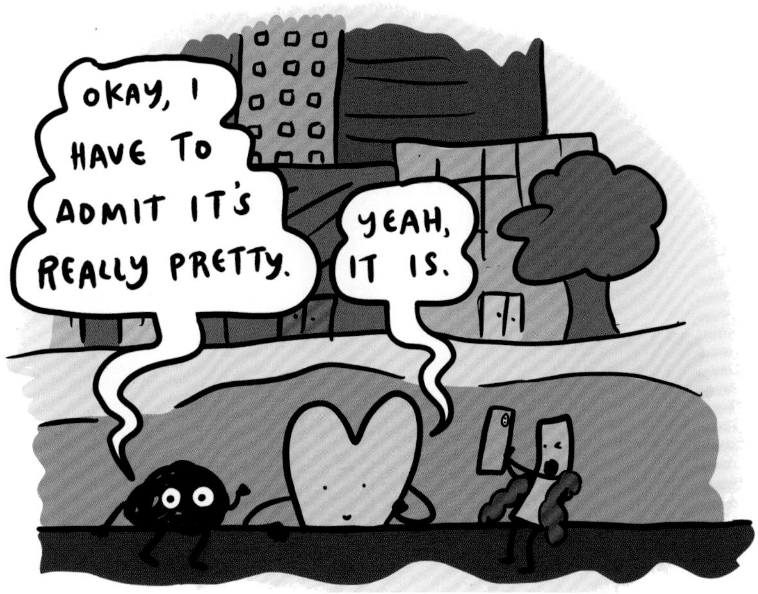
OKAY, I HAVE TO ADMIT IT'S REALLY PRETTY.
YEAH, IT IS.

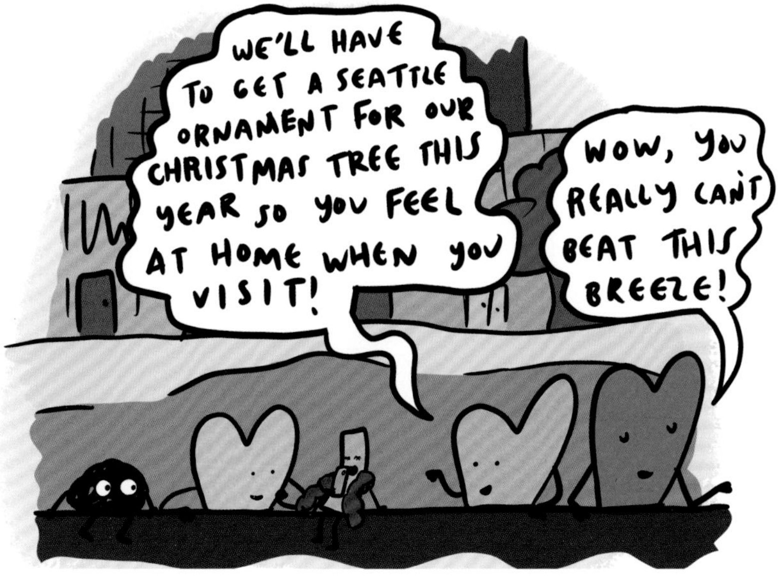
WE'LL HAVE TO GET A SEATTLE ORNAMENT FOR OUR CHRISTMAS TREE THIS YEAR SO YOU FEEL AT HOME WHEN YOU VISIT!
WOW, YOU REALLY CAN'T BEAT THIS BREEZE!

I knew that a lot stood before me—meeting my roommates, unpacking the garbage bags crammed in my trunk, crying as I hugged my parents goodbye, finding a job, learning the bus routes and neighborhoods and intricacies of a place so new. But for a moment longer, I was still on my way, not yet here, not totally. And there was something freeing about that.

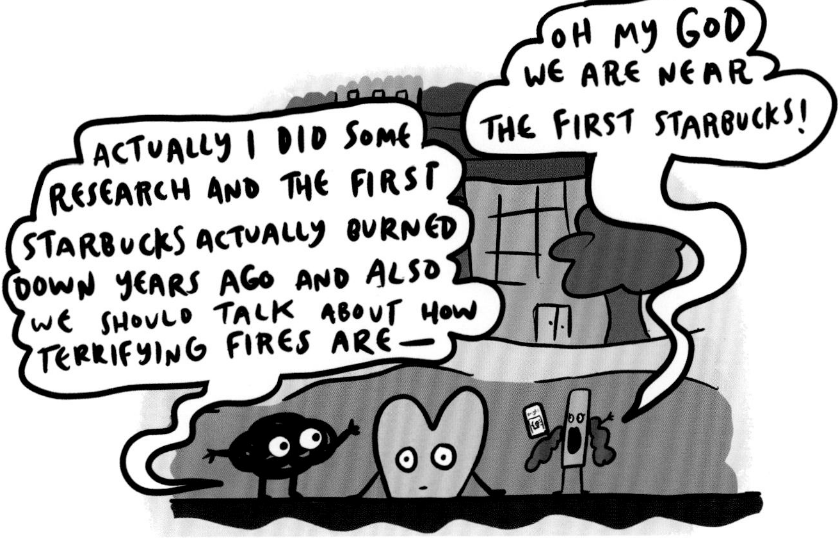
ACTUALLY I DID SOME RESEARCH AND THE FIRST STARBUCKS ACTUALLY BURNED DOWN YEARS AGO AND ALSO WE SHOULD TALK ABOUT HOW TERRIFYING FIRES ARE—
OH MY GOD WE ARE NEAR THE FIRST STARBUCKS!

I'd worry about it later.

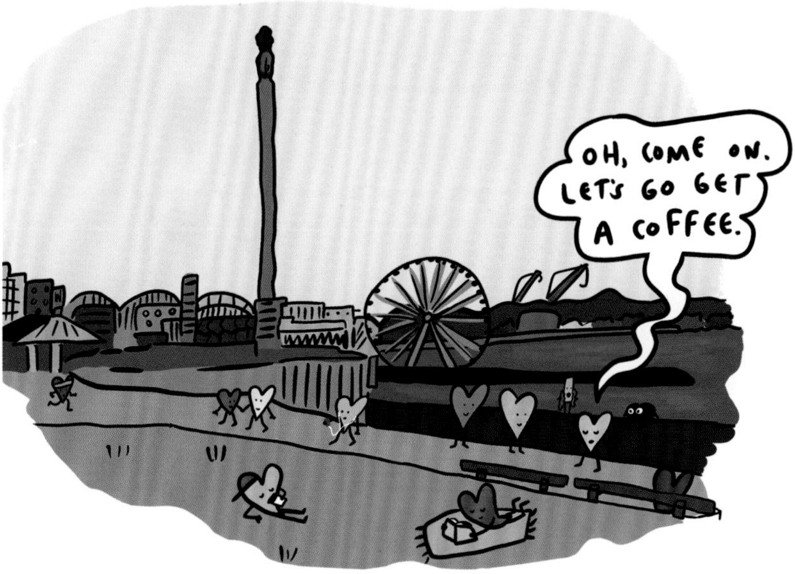
OH, COME ON. LET'S GO GET A COFFEE.

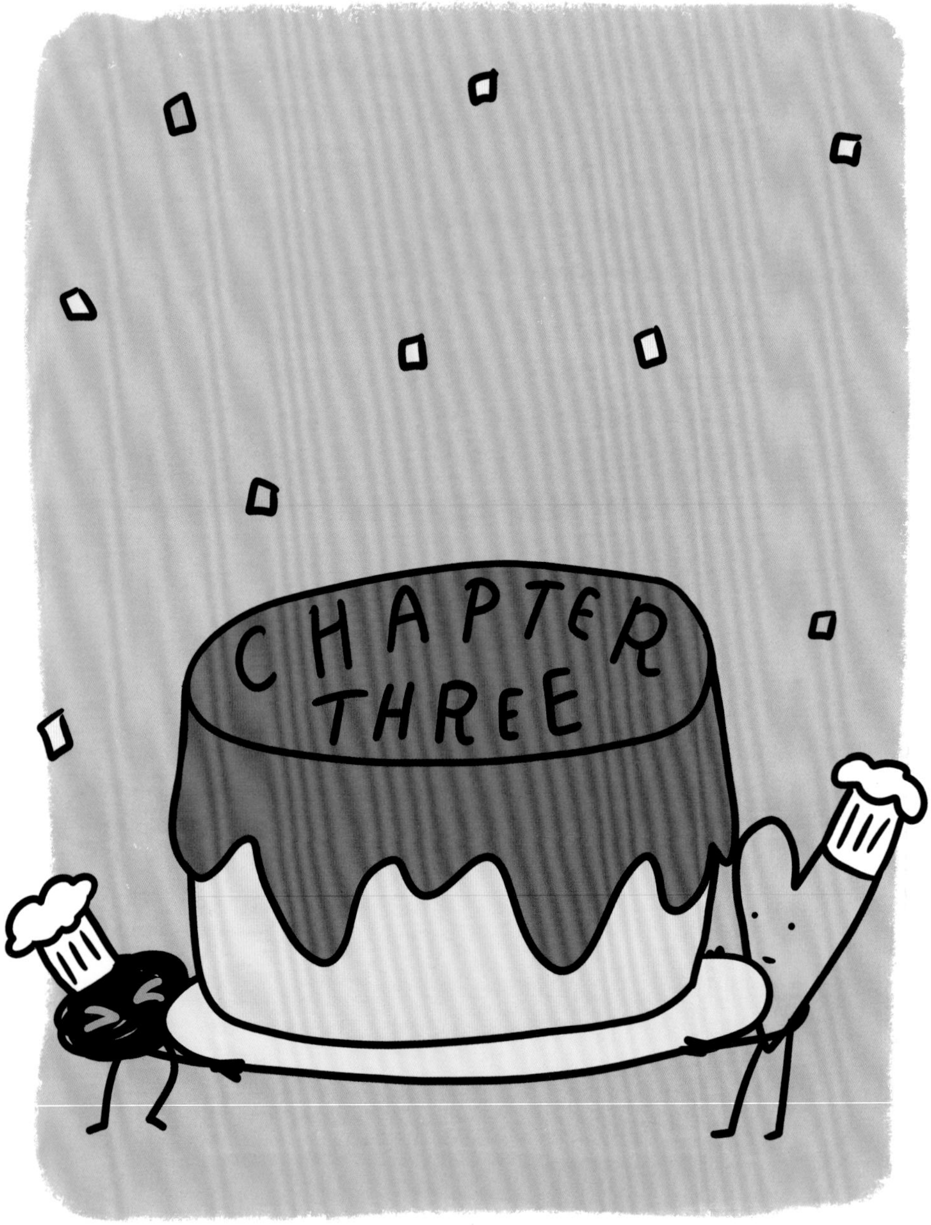
CHAPTER
THREE

As a kid, my goals for the future were admittedly shortsighted.

I was the oldest child in my family, so the idea of adolescence was almost mythical—something I saw only in movies or on nights we had a babysitter. And from what I gleaned, becoming a teenager was the gateway to independence. Teenagers went to the mall unsupervised! They passed notes in the hallway between classes! They wore cool clothes and had cell phones and maybe even called their crushes on them.

But during the summer before I started middle school, my fascination with adolescence veered into obsession. Like a caterpillar that wanted to skip the cocoon entirely, it was as if I was searching for a pair of butterfly wings to strap on and take flight.

Of course, skipping the cocoon wasn't an option, so I decided to practice being a teenager instead. I'd press tinfoil onto my teeth and pretend it was the work of an orthodontist.

I'd fold my tank tops halfway up while wearing them to create a pretend bra.

And when I was alone in my room, I would practice what I would say when I'd inevitably get asked out by someone after school.

I'd watch television shows about middle schoolers who had tight-knit friend groups and decorated lockers and love interests, and I'd envision all of this would be possible once I started sixth grade.

But then, puberty hit me like a thick wave of body spray in a school locker room: surprising, and too much at once.

I grew a few inches, my face became bumpier and redder, and my mom gently suggested I start wearing deodorant. Hairs started sprouting from parts of my body that made no sense, my mood whipped back and forth like a flag in a hurricane, and not even the health class I'd taken in fifth grade could prepare me for the extra weight that lightly padded my chest and hips. Worst of all, Anxiety started acting strange—stranger than usual.

Just as quickly as this surge of hormones arrived, so did the first day of sixth grade. My neighborhood sat smack in the middle of a school zoning line, which meant that most of my friends from elementary school would be going to one middle school while I'd head off to another one, where I'd know only a handful of other students. At first, this change seemed like a great opportunity for reinvention, but as I walked up the street to my bus stop, it felt like all my teenage aspirations were like grapes under the sun, shriveling into little raisins of self-consciousness.

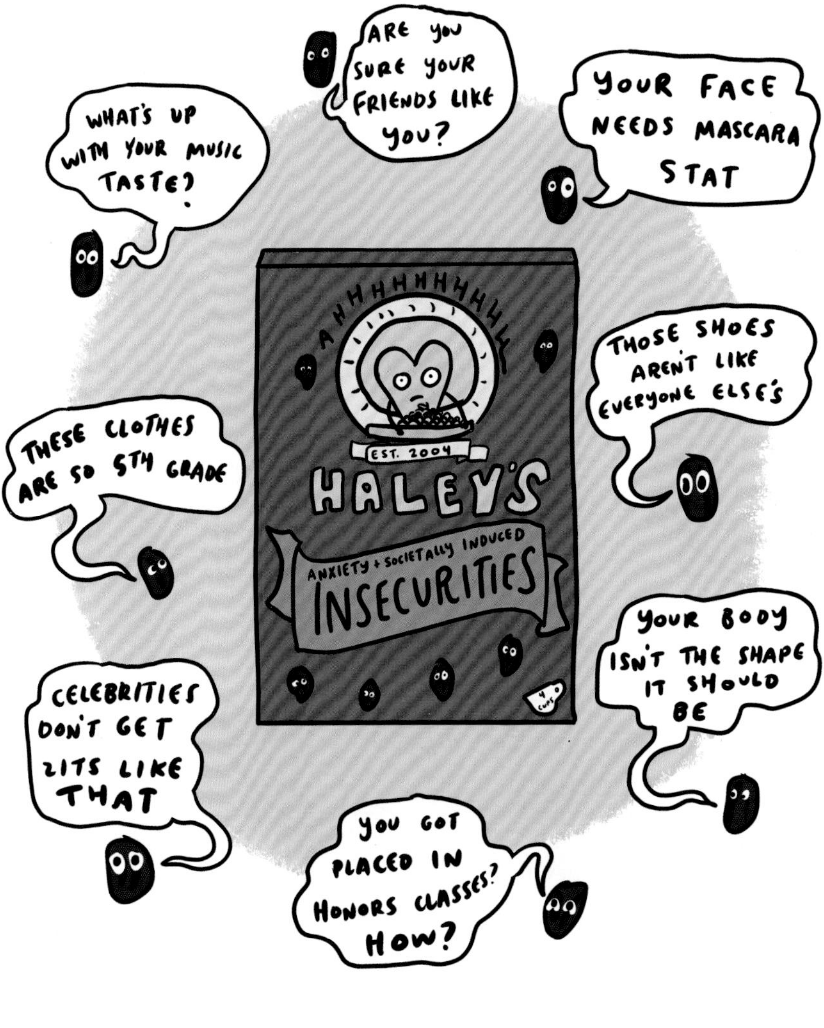
ARE YOU SURE YOUR FRIENDS LIKE YOU?
YOUR FACE NEEDS MASCARA STAT
WHAT'S UP WITH YOUR MUSIC TASTE?
AHHHHHHHHH
EST. 2004
HALEY'S
ANXIETY + SOCIETALLY INDUCED
INSECURITIES
THOSE SHOES AREN'T LIKE EVERYONE ELSE'S
THESE CLOTHES ARE SO 5TH GRADE
YOUR BODY ISN'T THE SHAPE IT SHOULD BE
CELEBRITIES DON'T GET ZITS LIKE THAT
YOU GOT PLACED IN HONORS CLASSES? HOW?

And once I arrived at the school itself, I was horrified to discover that middle school was nothing like the television shows I'd studied all summer long. The hallways were hot and crowded. The locker I'd been so excited to decorate was too narrow to fit all my textbooks. The bathrooms smelled like a nauseating mix of cheap perfume and urine, and my first two classes were taught by teachers who barely cracked a smile while sharing the course syllabus. But none of these horrors held a candle to what awaited me when the bell rang for lunch.

One step into the cafeteria proved that the few people I did know had other friends. The tables were crowded with friend groups, all of whom were laughing and comparing class schedules and trading snacks. I felt like I was treading water, surrounded by lifeboats at capacity—no room for one more. But I decided that begging for rescue sounded better than outright drowning.

My tray was shaking in my hands as I approached a table of girls, one of whom was on my summer league swim team. Then I uttered four of the scariest words known to tweens everywhere:

CAN I SIT HERE?

They were kind and nodded, but I noticed two of them exchange a look and then carry on their conversation as if I wasn't there. It was almost too excruciating to eat the bagel sandwich my mom had packed me.

But then, something happened.

At least, that's how I think the Liar arrived.

Don't get me wrong: I'd met the Liar before. When I was younger, we crafted some of my most convincing fibs.

These were lies that felt as if I'd plucked a sprinkle from a dough-nut and promised I hadn't touched it—sure, it wasn't the *truth*, but also, who would miss a sprinkle on a doughnut with, like, four hundred *other* sprinkles? It all felt harmless.

But lying about my interests? This felt like another doughnut situation entirely—like swearing my favorite kind was a cinnamon twist when what I truly wanted was a French cruller. And it didn't help that Anxiety was a little wary.

The Liar swore his intentions were totally and completely honorable.

And with that refresher, the Liar insisted we put his teachings into practice—starting with the conversation happening between the girls I'd chosen to sit with.

Anxiety wasn't too keen on this idea.

75

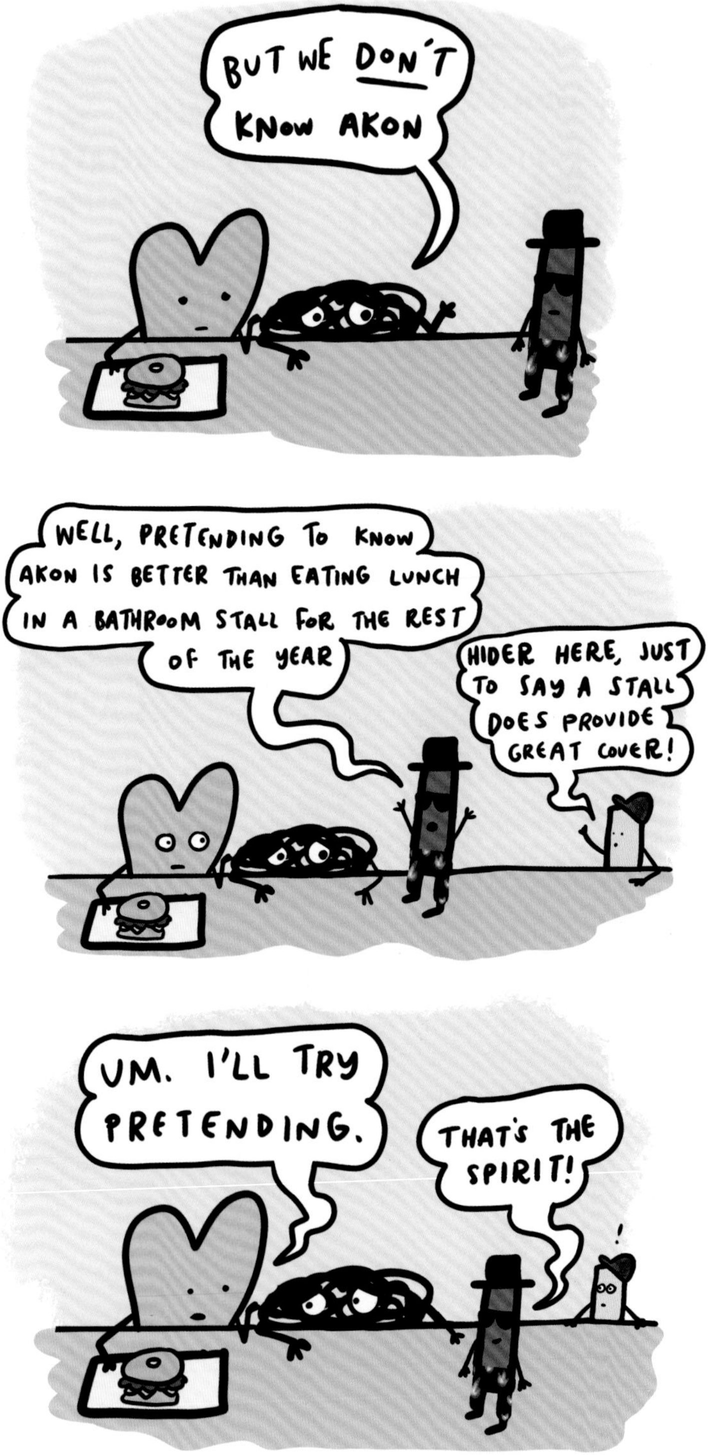
BUT WE DON'T KNOW AKON
WELL, PRETENDING TO KNOW AKON IS BETTER THAN EATING LUNCH IN A BATHROOM STALL FOR THE REST OF THE YEAR
HIDER HERE, JUST TO SAY A STALL DOES PROVIDE GREAT COVER!
UM. I'LL TRY PRETENDING.
THAT'S THE SPIRIT!
!

I began to sit at the edge of the lunch table each day, waiting for a moment I could insert myself in the conversation, swearing I listened to that band or saw that movie or had that designer necklace (I lost it at camp, I swear!). It almost felt like I was leveling up with each well-received lie, like I was doing surprisingly well on a tricky game-show.

At first, the lies I told were solely to impress others.

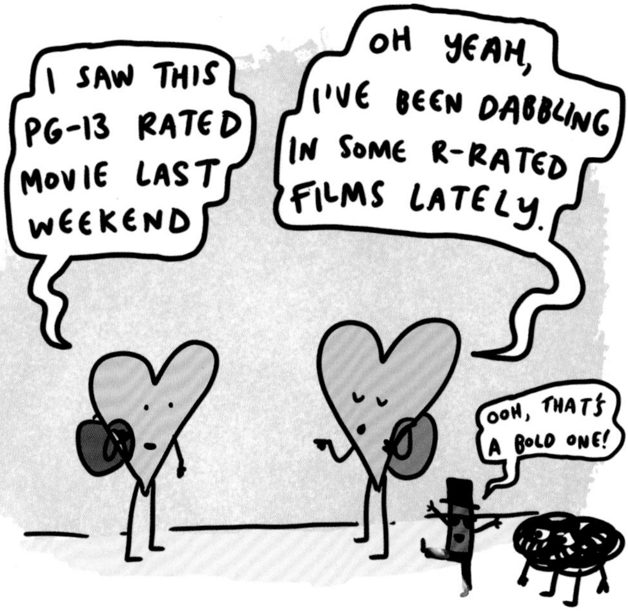
I SAW THIS PG-13 RATED MOVIE LAST WEEKEND
OH YEAH, I'VE BEEN DABBLING IN SOME R-RATED FILMS LATELY.
OOH, THAT'S A BOLD ONE!

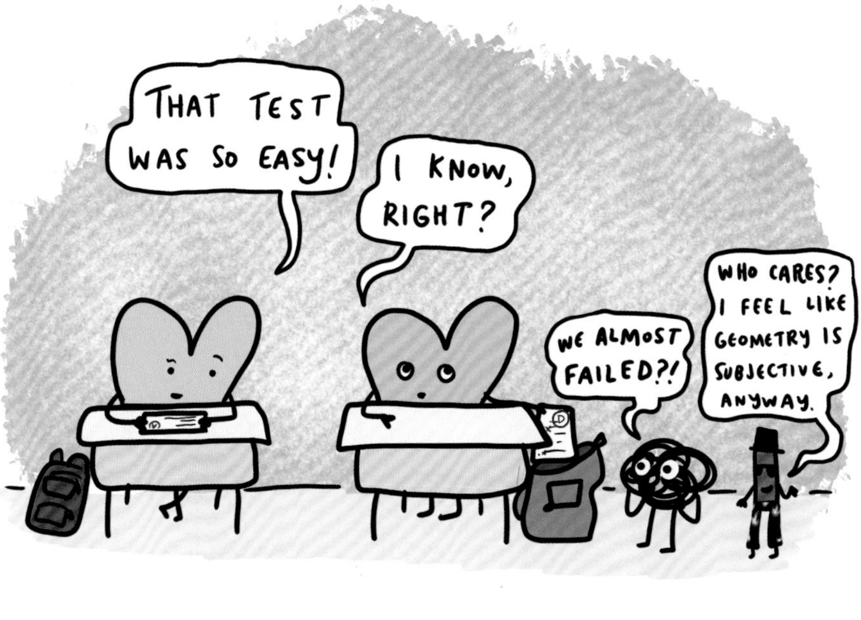
THAT TEST WAS SO EASY!
I KNOW, RIGHT?
WE ALMOST FAILED?!
WHO CARES? I FEEL LIKE GEOMETRY IS SUBJECTIVE, ANYWAY.

And sometimes, there were lies I told for no ascertainable reason, spurted out like a burst of confetti at the DMV—out of place and downright confusing.

Even though Anxiety was starting to feel stressed about how many stories we had to keep straight, the persona I was building seemed to be working—I was almost beginning to believe my own lies. When Ashley, one of the girls from the lunch table, invited me to her birthday party, it felt as if I was receiving an award for my efforts.

CERTIFICATE OF ACHIEVEMENT

THIS ACKNOWLEDGES THAT

*haley*

HAS SUCCESSFULLY BEEN INVITED TO HER FIRST MIDDLE SCHOOL PARTY

*The Liar*

SIGNED THE LIAR

The party was on a Saturday night at Ashley's house. My mom dropped me off with a gift-wrapped charm bracelet from the mall. Inside, Ashley's mother was sitting on the couch, watching reality television. "They're down there," she said, waving toward a door near the kitchen without breaking her gaze from the screen. As I descended the stairs, I couldn't help noticing that Ashley's basement didn't look like the birthday parties I'd been to in the past.

## WHAT I EXPECTED:

PASTEL DECORATIONS

CAKE (OUH!)

AN OPEN SEAT TO QUICKLY TAKE & BLEND IN

But there was none of that—no streamers, no bright party hats. And to make matters more terrifying, it wasn't just the girls from lunch like I thought it would be, but also some older kids I only recognized from the hallways during class change.

## WHAT THE PARTY ACTUALLY LOOKED LIKE:

7TH-GRADE BOYS (AHH!)

SNACKS

THE GIRLS FROM LUNCH

I stood at the base of the stairs, my brain barely computing the scene.

With the present gripped tightly to my chest, I walked over to Ashley, who was talking to one of the seventh-grade boys.

There is perhaps nothing more isolating than feeling alone in a crowd, especially if that crowd is a group of cool preteens in an unsupervised setting. At least, that's how I felt as I found a seat on the edge of the couch near the girls from lunch, waiting for an opportunity to chime in. But the energy felt different—more casual, and yet, more intimidating.

The Liar and Anxiety were both itching to advise my next move.

But the Liar was the one who had gotten me to this party in the first place, so I decided to take his advice.

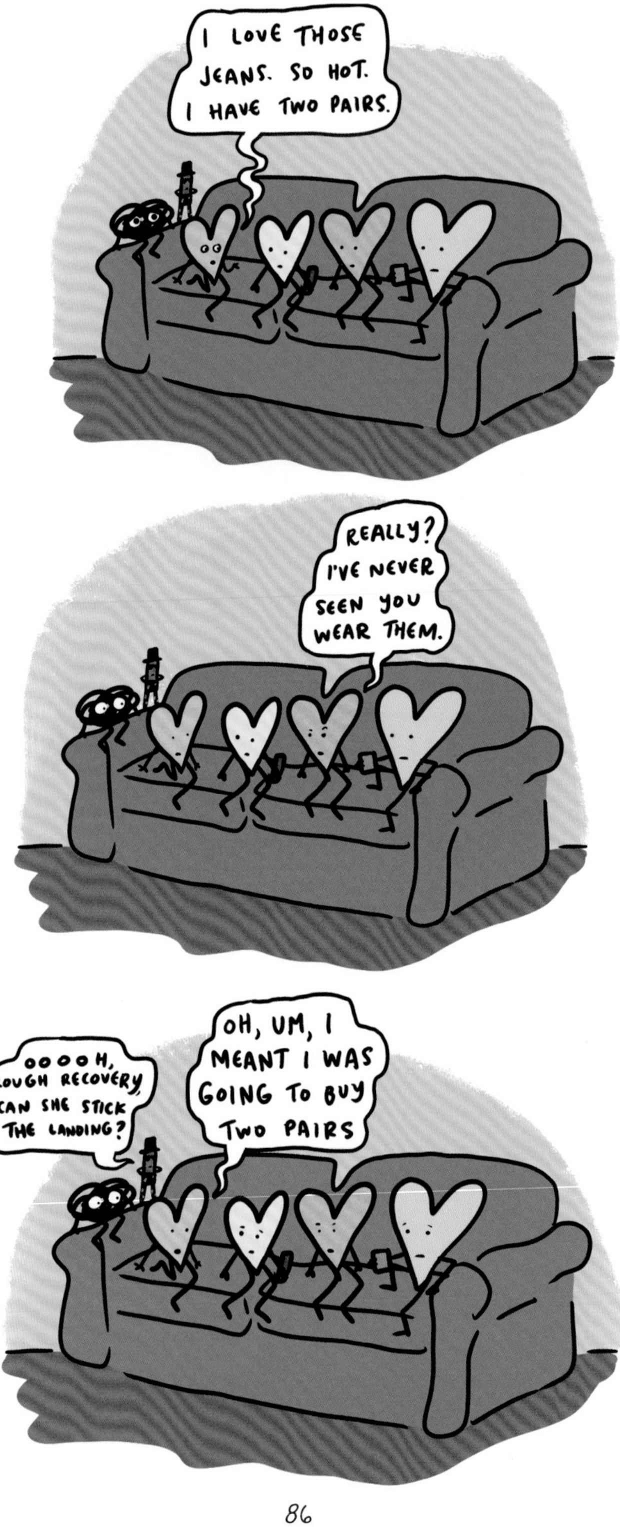
I LOVE THOSE JEANS. SO HOT. I HAVE TWO PAIRS.
REALLY? I'VE NEVER SEEN YOU WEAR THEM.
OOOOH, ROUGH RECOVERY, CAN SHE STICK THE LANDING?
OH, UM, I MEANT I WAS GOING TO BUY TWO PAIRS

It wasn't hard to choose who to listen to that time.

# PARTY SAFE SPACE:

Behind the locked door of the bathroom, we tried to figure out what went wrong.

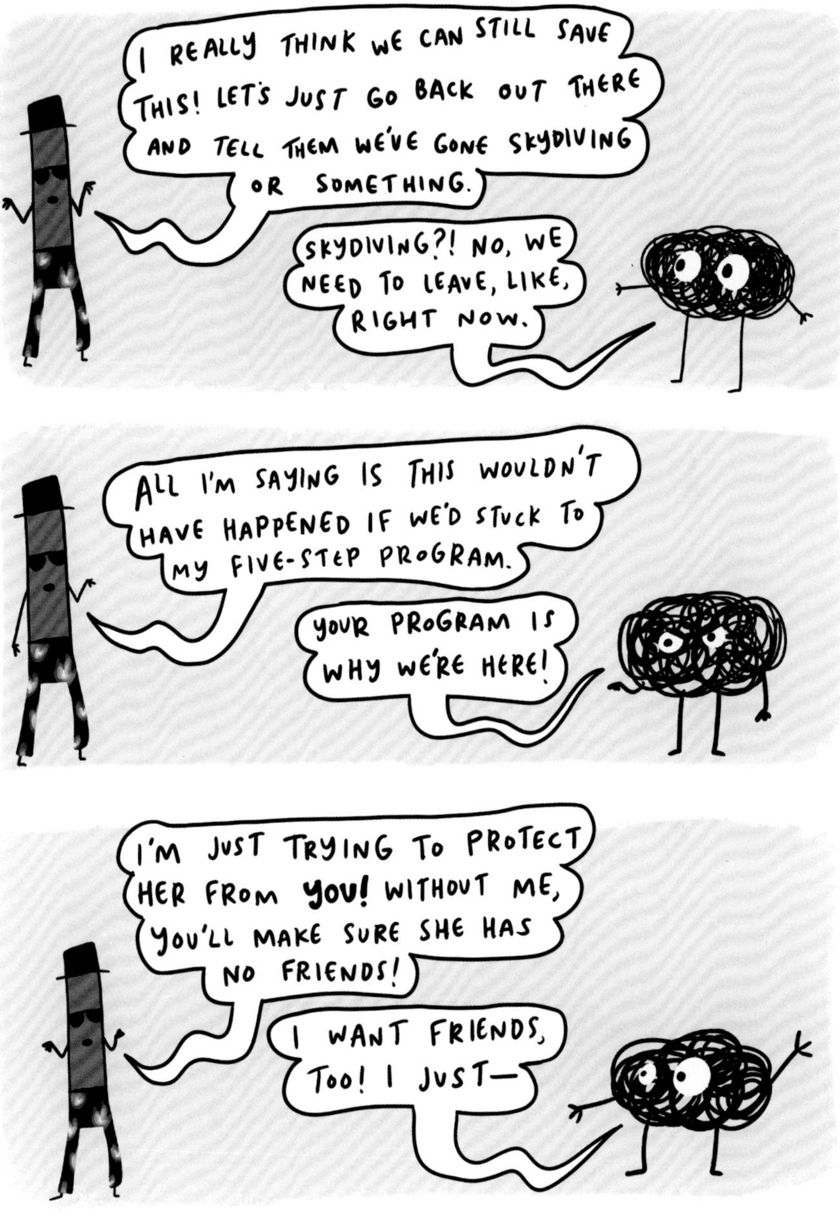
I REALLY THINK WE CAN STILL SAVE THIS! LET'S JUST GO BACK OUT THERE AND TELL THEM WE'VE GONE SKYDIVING OR SOMETHING.
SKYDIVING?! NO, WE NEED TO LEAVE, LIKE, RIGHT NOW.
ALL I'M SAYING IS THIS WOULDN'T HAVE HAPPENED IF WE'D STUCK TO MY FIVE-STEP PROGRAM.
YOUR PROGRAM IS WHY WE'RE HERE!
I'M JUST TRYING TO PROTECT HER FROM **YOU!** WITHOUT ME, YOU'LL MAKE SURE SHE HAS NO FRIENDS!
I WANT FRIENDS, TOO! I JUST—

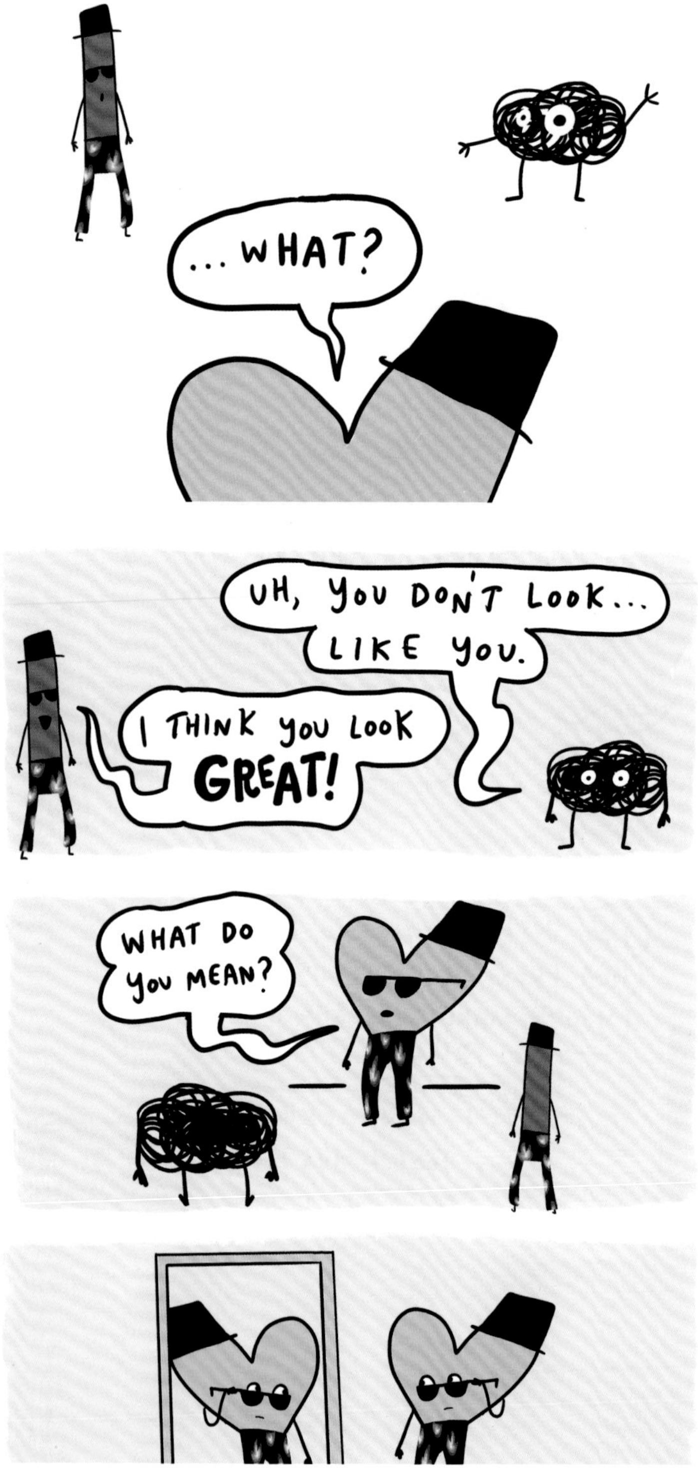
...WHAT?
UH, YOU DON'T LOOK... LIKE YOU.
I THINK YOU LOOK GREAT!
WHAT DO YOU MEAN?

I wish I could say that it was then, in the bathroom at Ashley's twelfth birthday party, that I realized lying was not a solution but more like a temporary mask—one that made me look ridiculous, but more importantly, not like myself—and that I stormed back into the party and gave a beautiful, heart-wrenching confession about how I'd been hiding this whole time, but this was the real me! Take it or leave it, folks!

But that's not how life works.

What I did do was call my mom and ask to be picked up.

At home, I tried not to think about how lunch would go on Monday, or Tuesday, or for the rest of the year. Instead, I went upstairs and sat in my bedroom and took comfort in all the things that had seemed too childish just earlier that day—my bright floral curtains, my favorite stuffed animal, even the little night-light by my bed.

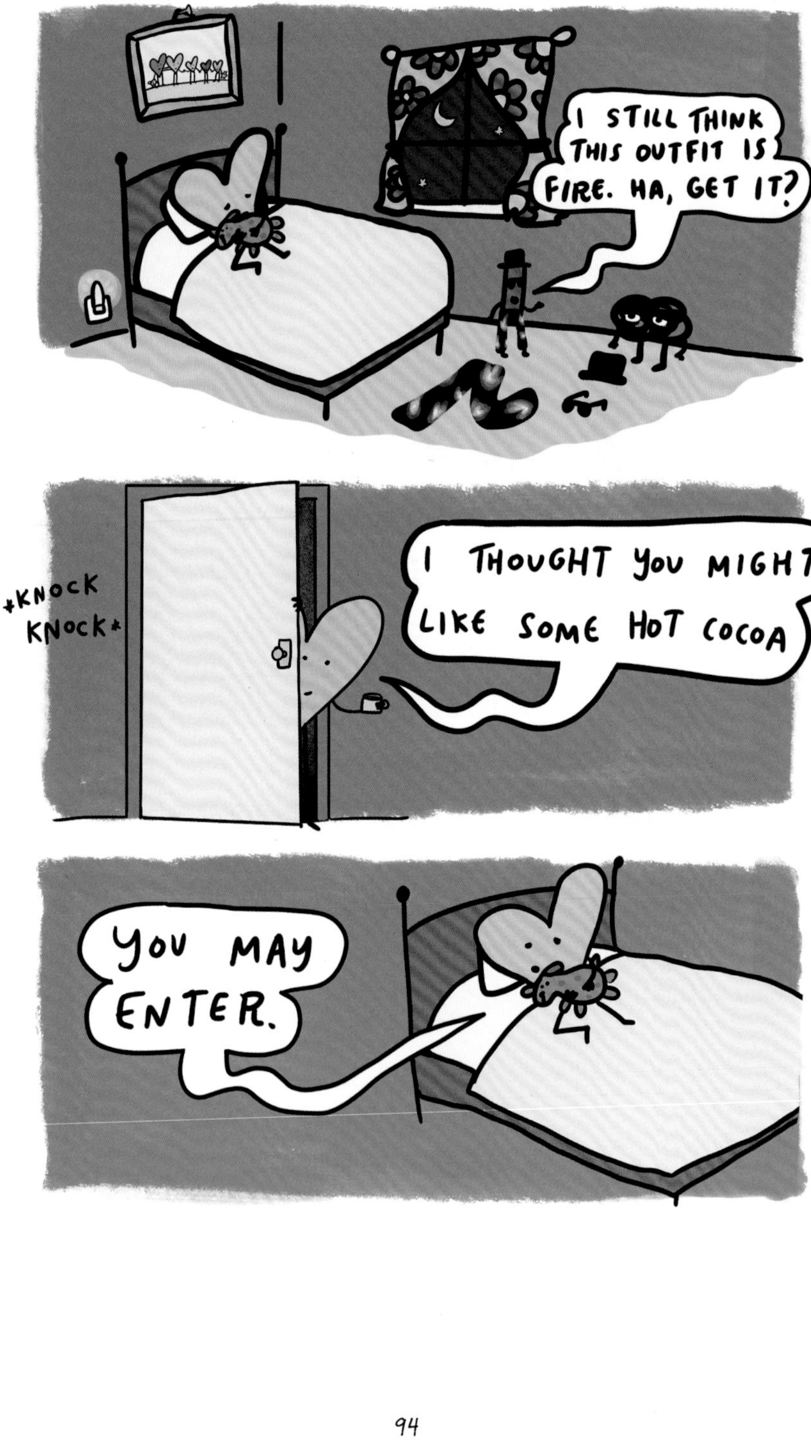
I STILL THINK THIS OUTFIT IS FIRE. HA, GET IT?
*KNOCK KNOCK*
I THOUGHT YOU MIGHT LIKE SOME HOT COCOA
YOU MAY ENTER.

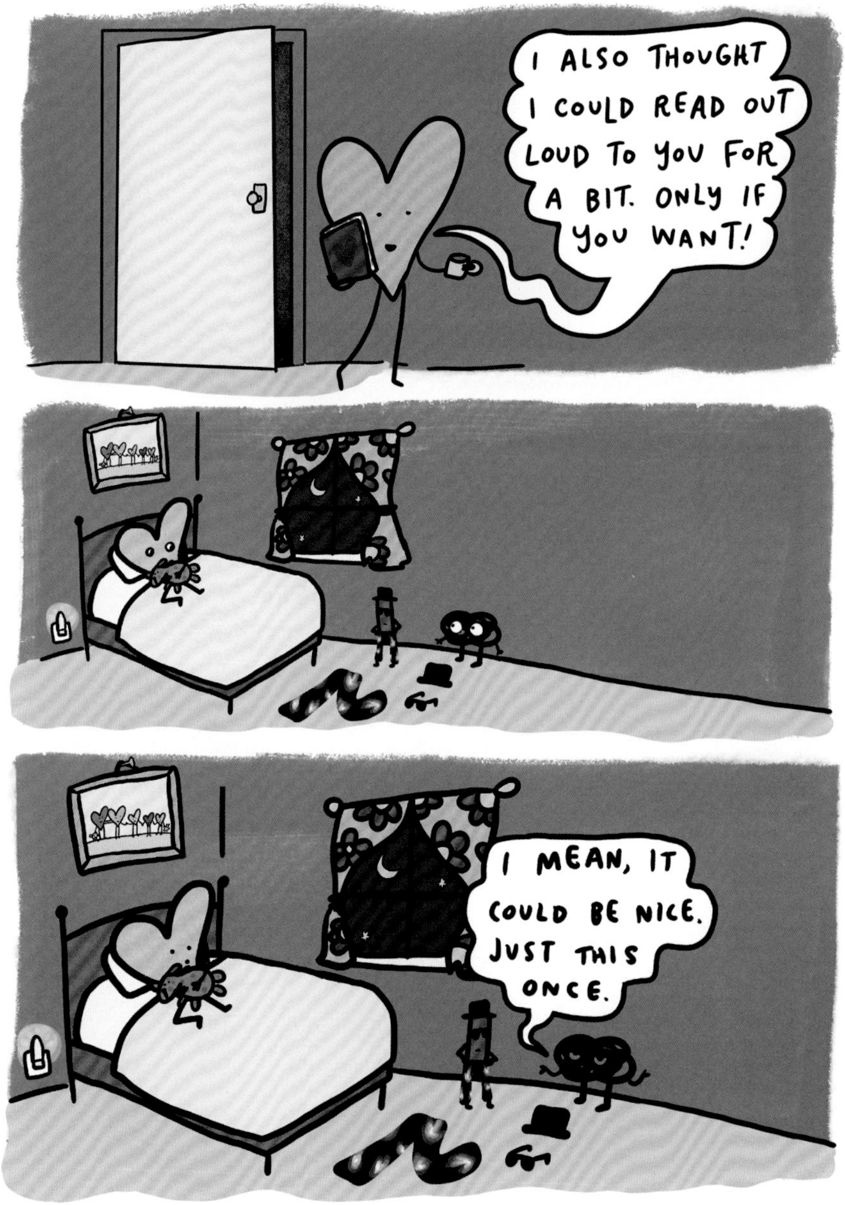
I ALSO THOUGHT I COULD READ OUT LOUD TO YOU FOR A BIT. ONLY IF YOU WANT!
I MEAN, IT COULD BE NICE. JUST THIS ONCE.

But even when you're an almost-cool preteen on track to being a definitely cool teenager, the childish stuff does make some of the scarier stuff disappear.

Even if just for a little bit.

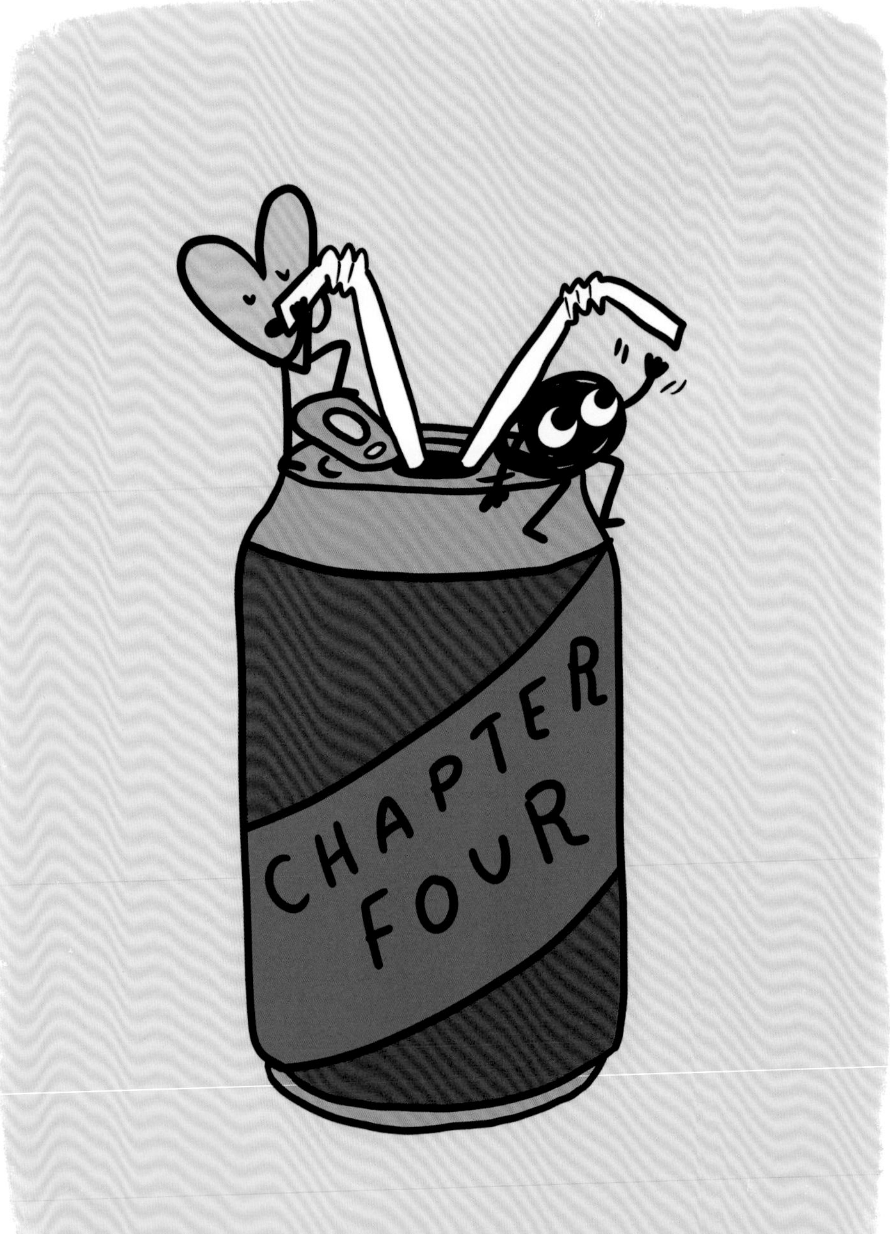
CHAPTER FOUR

The first time I got drunk was on a European river cruise.

FUN LIL BOAT

Let's be clear: this wasn't a wild, drink-till-you-can't-stand, MTV spring break kind of boat ride.

Instead, I was celebrating my high school graduation with my grandparents, and I brought down the average age on the boat by about thirty years.

It was our first night aboard, and we had just sat down for dinner when a waiter reached over my shoulder to pour me a hefty glass of white wine.

Here's the thing: I was terrified of drinking. I'm not sure when this fear initially took root—it might have been in fifth grade, when a police officer came to my classroom as a part of the DARE program.

Or maybe it was the disturbing drunk driving videos we watched in my driver's education course, each clip ending with cars crumpled on bloody pavement.

Or perhaps the fear solidified on the ultra-competitive year-round swim team I trained with for most of my childhood, where my coach would detail the horrors guaranteed with even a sip of alcohol. My teammates and I were required to sign contracts promising we wouldn't drink, and I had no problem scribbling my name across the dotted line.

That's because for the most part, I didn't mind my inexperience with drinking. I never sought out unsupervised house parties (it helped that I wasn't invited in the first place), and it didn't even cross my mind to raid my parents' liquor cabinet. My weekends were instead spent sleeping over at my friend Syd's house after Friday afternoon swim practice, our wildest nights filled with watching parody sci-fi movies and sneaking an extra piece of cake before bed.

Back on the cruise, however, my inexperience felt kind of embarrassing—and it would only be more embarrassing in a few weeks, when I'd head off to a small liberal arts college in rural Pennsylvania. Aside from the fact that I'd be competing for the school's swim team and maybe majoring in English, it felt impossible to envision what my life would look like there.

For a moment, I wondered if it was this impending life change or the waves beneath the river cruise that left my stomach churning. Regardless, I made eye contact with Anxiety and took a long pull from the wineglass, half-sure an alarm would go off to announce my underage activity.

But as the alcohol settled into my system, I found that talking to the strangers we were sharing a table with was suddenly not so daunting. It was as if my personality had been steeped in charisma: my stories sounded better, my laugh came easily, and when the waiter came back around to top off my glass, I wondered if I'd unlocked the secret to a more likable version of myself. I felt lighter, as if I was levitating above the ground, no longer responsible for carrying all of me.

A month later at my first college party, I was desperate to re-create that weightlessness.

I stood in the unfinished basement of an off-campus house, clutching a plastic red cup and watching some sophomores play beer pong. It was the swim team's first party of the year, and I kept bumping shoulders with the other freshmen, all of us clumped together like sheep herded in a corner. We'd only been there for twenty minutes, and I'd already fumbled through all of my conversation starters.

I tried to look comfortable, but all I could think about was how much this scene contrasted from the parties I'd seen depicted in movies. Instead of strobe lights or strands of holiday lights or even a neon beer sign, the only light in the room came from a lone bulb hanging above the pong table, and I couldn't tell if it was the dampness in the air or the nervous sweat collecting in my armpits that left me shivering. A cheap speaker was propped on a stack of crates, spitting out a loud party anthem about drinking brand-name tequila and feeling young and wild and free.

From those movies I watched growing up, parties were supposed to be plot thickeners. It was at a party that you could have a heated argument or state a bold declaration or even win an iconic dance battle. You could tell your secrets to a stranger in line for the bathroom or bump into a potential love interest on the stairs or even do a righteous keg stand in front of a cheering crowd.

But the plot at this party was developing slowly, if at all. My brain felt blank, as if the switch controlling my social skills had been flipped off.

Upstairs, there was a group of juniors in the living room, where everyone seemed to know the words to the bass-heavy song blaring from yet another set of speakers. A few seniors stood in the kitchen, laughing about something that happened at a swim meet two years ago. As I cut through a maze of slurred conversations and half-filled cups, I felt even more out of place than I had downstairs.

It felt like I was wearing my inexperience like a heavy coat in summertime, and I wondered if everyone could tell I was unversed in what seemed like a widely shared language.

I was about to reprise my favorite party trick of hiding in the bathroom when someone called out to me.

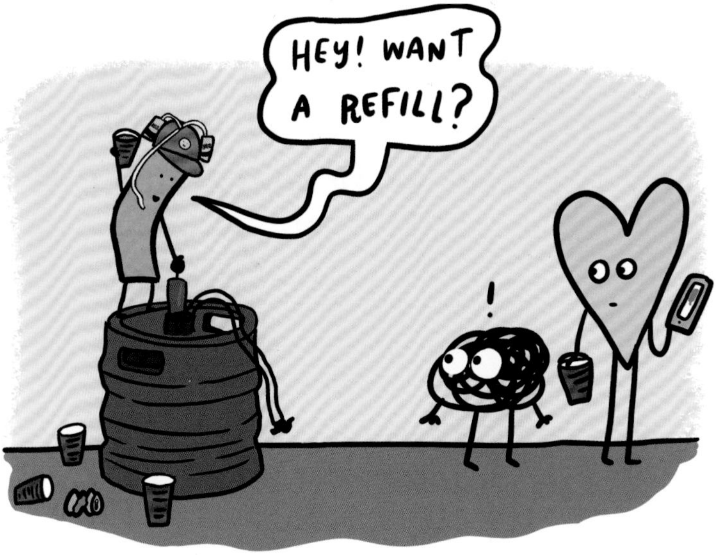
HEY! WANT A REFILL?

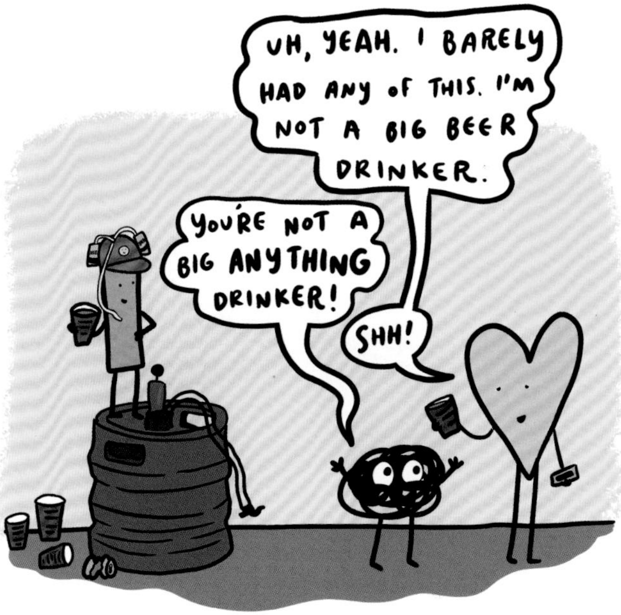
UH, YEAH. I BARELY HAD ANY OF THIS. I'M NOT A BIG BEER DRINKER.
YOU'RE NOT A BIG ANYTHING DRINKER!
SHH!

I watched as the stranger pulled a cup from the kitchen counter and dipped it into a massive trash can filled with bright purple liquid, not unlike a potion brewing in a witch's cauldron.

I winced as a sour burn hit the back of my throat, but the sickly sweet flavor quickly overpowered the scorch of liquor.

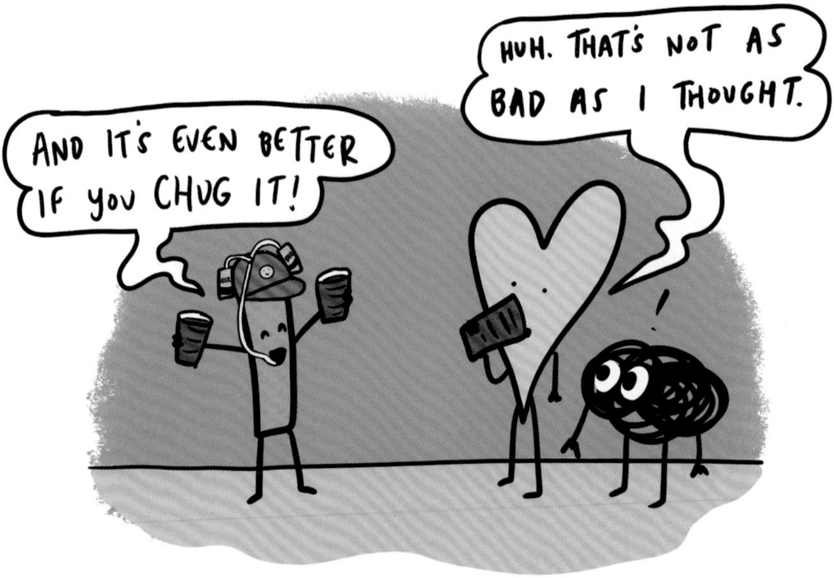
AND IT'S EVEN BETTER IF YOU CHUG IT!
HUH. THAT'S NOT AS BAD AS I THOUGHT.

So I did.

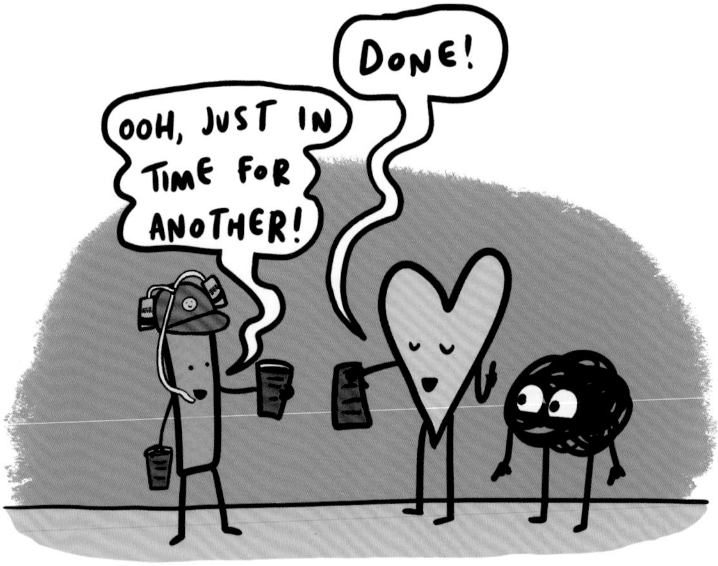
DONE!
OOH, JUST IN TIME FOR ANOTHER!

And with that he disappeared into a group of people congregating by the keg. I took a long sip from my cup, avoiding Anxiety's eyes as I scrolled through my new friend's profile.

It didn't take long for the juice to take effect in my body, and soon I felt even more buoyant than I had on that river cruise. The music sounded better, the room felt brighter, and when I caught my eye in the mirror, I even thought I looked better, face flushed and eyes sparkling.

Maybe I did feel dizzy, but I ignored it when I saw the Partier waving to me from the other room.

The Partier and I became fast friends that night. We returned to the trash can a few more times, where I dunked my cup in and rubbed my wet hands on my jeans. We played drinking games I'd never heard of—I was terrible at all of them but didn't feel the usual flush of embarrassment I otherwise might have. I squinted into the flash of the camera as we posed for photos in front of a faded American flag pinned to the wall, and when the Partier pulled me onto the coffee table as his favorite song came on, it was as if I had fully shed the insecurity I'd worn just a few hours ago. Best of all, every time I took another sip, Anxiety seemed to get quieter.

When the party ended and the swim house cleared out, the Partier led the way to a fraternity house, where the front porch was lined with some of the guys who lived there.

Inside, we giggled at our reflections in the bathroom, the sounds of the dance floor muffled through the door. And when we joined the dance floor ourselves, it felt as if the music was swallowing me whole—and I would have let it if it tried. I marveled at how numb my nose was to the touch, how warm my cheeks were, how good the bodies of strangers felt as they grazed my own, how utterly invincible I felt.

But most of all, I loved how faint Anxiety's usual comments were.

As I flopped into my bed that night, my phone dinged with a notification from the Partier, who had already uploaded photos from the night to Facebook. I scrolled through them, grateful for proof that I hadn't made it all up in my head.

After clumsily plugging my phone into its charger, I stared at the popcorn ceiling, mesmerized by how the bumps seemed to move even though I was perfectly still.

I woke up the next morning to stark sunlight against the cinder-block walls of my dorm. There was no sign of the hangover I'd seen referenced in films—maybe I didn't want my life to be too much like the movies after all.

I met a few of the freshman swimmers at the dining hall for breakfast, recounting the details of our night over plates of scrambled eggs and coffee.

At first, Anxiety did try to let me enjoy it, backing off as I spent almost every free hour with my new friends. We sprawled out on the floor in one of our dorm rooms and took online quizzes.

We tried on sweatshirts in the school bookstore, debating whether our school colors were flattering or terrible.

We got overpriced iced coffee from the cute shop in town and walked around campus, laughing as we predicted what would happen during our next night out.

Though I knew college was a lot more than the social scene, it was hard to think about anything else. But when the semester soon crowded my schedule with classes and swim meets and library study sessions, Anxiety fell back in step, following me around like a shadow.

I was willing to live with it, because I knew exactly what—or rather, who—would quiet him down come the weekend.

The Partier would have spent the entire week party hopping, but my status as a collegiate athlete kept me in line. After all, we weren't allowed to go out during the forty-eight hours leading up to our Saturday swim meets.

But that just meant we went *all out* on Saturday nights. Each weekend fell into a similar rhythm: After our swim meet, I'd return to my dorm to take a nap. Then I'd meet my friends at the dining hall for dinner, followed by the mad dash to get ready. This routine entailed piling into one of our dorms, blaring a party playlist on shuffle, opening trays of blush and eyeshadow in front of mirrors, and retrieving hidden bottles of liquor from the back of a closet, mixing heavy pours with ice and soda from the vending machine. We'd carefully consider each of our outfits and take a shot with our noses pinched shut before heading to the swim house, tipsy enough to walk across campus in late autumn without a jacket.

And from there, the pattern only continued. We played the same games, drunkenly sang the same songs, and sucked down mouthfuls of the same too-sweet juice from the same trash can. The only real variant in the night was where we'd end up. Sometimes it was one of the fraternities on campus. Other times it was back to a dorm room, where the Partier suggested I drink some more. And every once in a while, we'd end up at the diner in town, eating pancakes while surrounded by fellow students in a drunken stupor.

My vocabulary expanded with each night out: a "pregame" was drinking before the party, "shotgunning" was piercing a can of shitty beer with a key and chugging the entire thing through the jagged hole, a "fracket" was a cheap jacket to wear (and lose) at fraternity houses and, as I learned firsthand just a month and a half after arriving to school, "blacking out" meant drinking so much that your memory of the night before came back in pieces, or not at all.

The first time I blacked out would have been more alarming if I hadn't been waiting for it to happen. I remember sitting in the dining hall just weeks prior, listening to older teammates recall stories of ridiculous nights from years past, ones that ended with sloppy hook-ups and lost memories and sometimes even a run-in with campus security. But these stories weren't told to be precautionary. They were legendary.

My first blackout, however, was no legend in the making. It was mid-October, and a group of us were pregaming in a dorm room on a Saturday night. We took shots, we danced, we took more shots, we sang, and the next thing I knew, I was in my bed, waking up with no recollection of how I got there.

At breakfast later that morning, I was comforted to hear that I had just knocked back one too many, that my friends had walked me home and tucked me into bed.

And for most of that semester, I really believed that. It was *just* sips: sips of warm beer, sips of sugary boxed wine (best enjoyed directly from the spout), sips of mixed drinks through thin straws, sips from shot glasses lined up on someone's desk, sips from the nozzle of the keg while being held upside down, sips earned during a game of flip cup, slap cup, anything with a cup, really. The more I sipped, the more my confidence grew. The more I sipped, the more Anxiety shrank.

131

But every night ended, and Anxiety was always waiting at the edge of my bed the next morning, wide-eyed and ready to obsessively review the events of the evening prior.

Truth be told, I wasn't worried. It was early winter, and things were going almost too well. I was somehow swimming faster than I had in years, I was on track to make the dean's list, and after spending most of my time with them, my friends felt more like family.

But more than anything, I believed I'd become a master party-goer.

For a while, this facade worked. When Anxiety voiced his concern about the fact that I barely remembered who left the hickey blooming on my neck or recalled how I cracked my phone screen or how I neglected to set an alarm after a Sunday night out and missed class, I just waved him off.

I slogged through exams knowing that there'd be drinking on the other side. I spent the holiday break listening to the songs I'd discovered at pregames and parties, daydreaming about hearing them in a basement again. And on our swim team training trip in January, the main motivator that got me through the two-a-day practices was knowing we could go out to the local bar that night, where pineapple-and-rums were two for one. The swim team had a brief dry season, during which we weren't supposed to go out or drink at all in anticipation of our championship meet at the end of February. When we won, I exhaled, finally on the other side of it. Life felt like it had finally begun for me, that this was the beginning of everything.

And it *was* the beginning of everything. Kind of.

All season, the upperclassmen on the team had been talking about how much fun the days and weeks and months after our championship meet were, starting with a fraternity party to celebrate the end of the season.

All the normal *I'm drunk!* feelings washed over me, and the excitement of the victory paired with the continued longing to fit in only led to me agreeing to more shots, more beers, more sips.

When I woke up the next morning, both my memories of the night before and my phone were missing. I pulled out my laptop and opened it to a Facebook status clearly written by one of the fraternity brothers.

But this morning, it was harder to agree with the Partier's blasé response, and my chest tightened with embarrassment when I saw that a lot of people from both college and my hometown had liked or commented on the post.

I would eventually learn that "hangxiety" was not a freak occurrence, but rather an expected presence after a night of heavy drinking. Things look different through sober eyes—you realize that maybe you shouldn't have taken that shot or danced with that person or left your phone wedged in the couch cushions at a party.

But I didn't have time to learn that lesson now.

Later that morning, I walked through the doorway of the frat house and immediately noticed how different the interior looked in the harsh daylight. The sticky floors reflected the glare of fluorescent lighting, picture frames hung crooked on the walls, but what was most disheveled of all was the brothers, slouched on the forest-green couches as if their batteries had been removed with the sun's arrival.

My phone was on a table, the screen even more fragmented than it had been before. As I retrieved it, a few guys laughed.

I felt like I was on a walk of shame as I left, one where my pride felt just as shattered as my phone screen.

But even still, I was desperate to drown out Anxiety's voice and any feelings of humiliation.

The nights out that followed only got sloppier. There was the time I threw up on the couch in the swim house on a Monday, and the time I told a classmate I was too sick to study with her, opting instead to take my textbook to a party. I found out later she had tried to drop soup off at my dorm, only to find I wasn't in bed after all. There was even the time when I stumbled across the quad, somehow avoiding campus security as I hugged a fifth of pomegranate vodka to my chest. My grades began slipping, but I didn't notice. My mind was set on the next party, the next time I could prove to everyone I belonged. It was like the easiest math problem in the world: add some alcohol, and my value changed for the better.

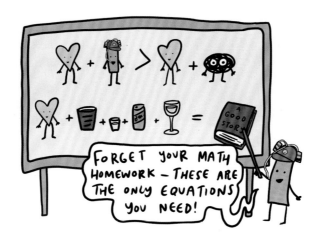

And even though going out meant I woke up the next day tired and unable to fully parse the previous night together, at least I was in my own bed.

But one weekend in late March, I woke up somewhere else.

It was a steady beeping that first stirred me. I groaned, wondering if I'd drunkenly set an alarm the night before, but then I opened my eyes to the sterile white walls of a hospital room.

My mind was racing as I tried to piece together the previous night. I'd pregamed in a friend's room, where we ate Goldfish crackers between shots, and I'd borrowed a black-and-white-striped dress—where was that dress? I looked down at the light blue hospital gown tied loosely at my neck and twice more down my spine. We'd gone to an off-campus party, and then what? My head felt heavy, and when I realized I was still drunk, I let out a panicked laugh.

"Oh, you're awake." A nurse walked in, flipping a piece of paper over her clipboard.

In short, yes, I was. The nurse handed me a yellow slip of paper, explaining it was an underage drinking citation from the police. I needed to sign and return it to the borough as soon as possible. She also handed me a sealed plastic bag with my dress, phone, shoes, and keys wedged like Tetris pieces inside.

Her unfazed demeanor made me think she'd seen this very scene many times before, that she was probably sick of dealing with the spoiled drunk kids from the preppy private college on the edge of town, kids who chugged energy drinks mixed with vodka, kids who eventually ran into a public safety officer and ended up here, in this examination room with its desolate walls and stark white beds. Stick a catheter between the legs, an IV in the arm, the heels in a bag, and it's just another day.

After confirming that my friends could come pick me up, I stood in the emergency room parking lot, my hair like a bird's nest on my head and my cheeks stained black, a mix of tears and smeared mascara.

But I was thinking about my reputation—about what everyone would think about me when they found out I wasn't the cool girl I had tried so hard to become, the kind who could knock back shots after doing a keg stand, still able to walk in a straight line.

When my friend's familiar blue car pulled around the bend, I felt my chest tighten, releasing only when my friends nearly fell out of the car, running to hug me before helping me into the back seat.

The next few days were a blur with a few standout moments. There was the call with my parents, their concern palpable even over the phone. There was the meeting with the dean of college life, who explained that I was granted medical amnesty but that if this happened again, major consequences would be on the table. There was the conversation in my swim coach's office, where I stared down at my knees, unable to believe we'd exchanged high fives at the championship swim meet just a month ago. And there was the slow piecing together of what had happened, compiled from teammates and dorm mates and classmates.

*Unlucky.* I clung to that word, assuring myself that's all my hospital visit had been: terrible, terrible luck. I guess that's why, when the Partier suggested we prove that we could have the comeback of the century the following weekend, I agreed, hoping a night back on the scene would push my hospital visit out of sight.

If the story went the way that eighteen-year-old Haley and the Partier wanted it to go, the rest of freshman year (and college, for that matter) would be a long string of proof that the hospital visit was a fluke, that I'd just had a little too much liquid courage.

But when I woke up in the hospital again less than a month later, it quickly became clear that wasn't the case.

For all I knew, it could've been a time loop—it was the same white room, the same monotonous beeping, the same hospital gown. But this time, I ripped the IV out of my arm and got out of bed, my balance immediately proving to be off-kilter.

And the terrible time loop continued. I got another citation from the borough, and learned I'd had another horrifying alcohol content percentage in my blood when I arrived at the hospital. The nurse handed me another plastic bag of my belongings zipped tight, and I waited outside for another ride back to campus in last night's outfit.

WHAT'S IN MY BAG: HOSPITAL EDITION

UNSETTLING PAPERWORK

CITATION

WEAVER, H
BAC: .28%

LAST NIGHT'S DRESS, WEIRDLY DAMP

PHONE (NO BATTERY)

KEYS (THANK GOD)

MISSING: AN EARRING, MEMORIES, DIGNITY

I was terrified to learn how I'd ended up at the hospital again—my memories were splintered as usual, starting and ending with the pregame I'd attended the day before. It had been an "Around the World" party, where we traveled to different dorms and off-campus houses, taking a shot at each. I'd done that and more—a whole can of beer chugged through a funnel, a mixed drink with a heart-shaped ice cube, a long sip sucked directly from a keg nozzle. That's when everything went dark, like an abrupt cliff disrupting a long road.

But I also remember Anxiety's voice being louder than usual. He had been more vocal at parties since the first hospital visit.

By the time I made it from the hospital back to my dorm, it was late morning. I trudged up the three flights of stairs to my room, grateful to find it empty.

My parents, understandably, were horrified. My BAC, higher this time, put me in a range dangerous enough to result in serious injury or even death. I heard my mom sniffle as my dad, in a heartbreakingly small voice, asked: Hadn't I learned from the last time?

I definitely hadn't. My thoughts were trained not on the danger of my actions, but rather on the danger of my social status.

# MY PRIORITIES, CIRCA APRIL 2012

The day trudged along, continuing to mirror the aftermath of the previous hospital visit. Emails showed up in my inbox—first from the dean, then from my coach, both requesting another meeting with me. My phone pinged with texts from friends, asking if I was okay. I wanted to respond, "What do you think?" but instead tried to play it cool.

I collected fragments of the night slowly. A friend came over and sat on my bed with me, gently recounting what she'd seen me drink, who she saw me kiss, and even which senior swimmer carried me back to my dorm after noticing that I couldn't stand up on my own. In the privacy of my resident advisor's room, I learned that my poor roommate had found me passed out on the bed, unresponsive. I learned that she quickly went to our resident advisor for help, that the ambulance was soon parked outside the dorm, its emergency lights illuminating the street like strobe lights in a nightclub. I learned that I was carted out on a stretcher as my dorm mates watched from their doorways, brought down three flights of stairs, and whisked away to the place I swore I'd never go again. This wasn't unlucky anymore. This was a pattern.

If my freshman year had been a snowball rolling down a mountain, slowly picking up ice and dirt as it gained momentum, this day felt like the collapse at the bottom of the hill, the tightly packed snow loosening and spilling out in every direction. I couldn't hold it together anymore.

At my first meeting with the dean earlier that month, I'd learned there would be major repercussions should I ever have an alcohol-related hospital visit again. But I had been barely listening, instead thinking of how I would manage the potential damage this incident would place upon my reputation. I guess that's why, when I sat in her office for the second time in a thirty-day span, my mouth dropped as she explained what would happen next.

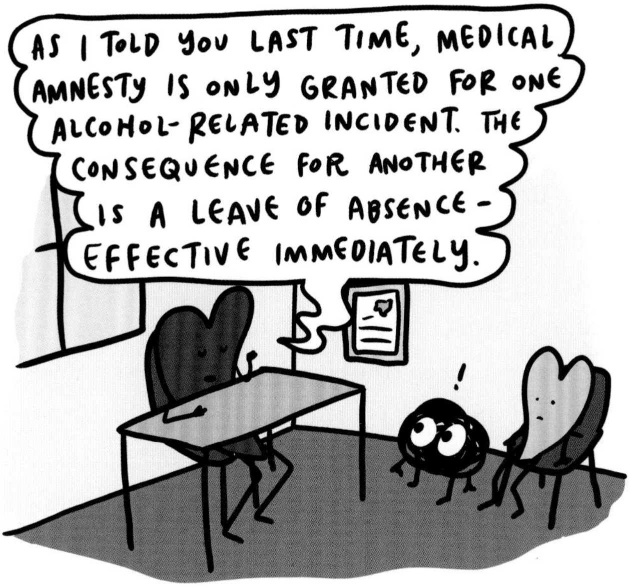
AS I TOLD YOU LAST TIME, MEDICAL AMNESTY IS ONLY GRANTED FOR ONE ALCOHOL-RELATED INCIDENT. THE CONSEQUENCE FOR ANOTHER IS A LEAVE OF ABSENCE—EFFECTIVE IMMEDIATELY.
!

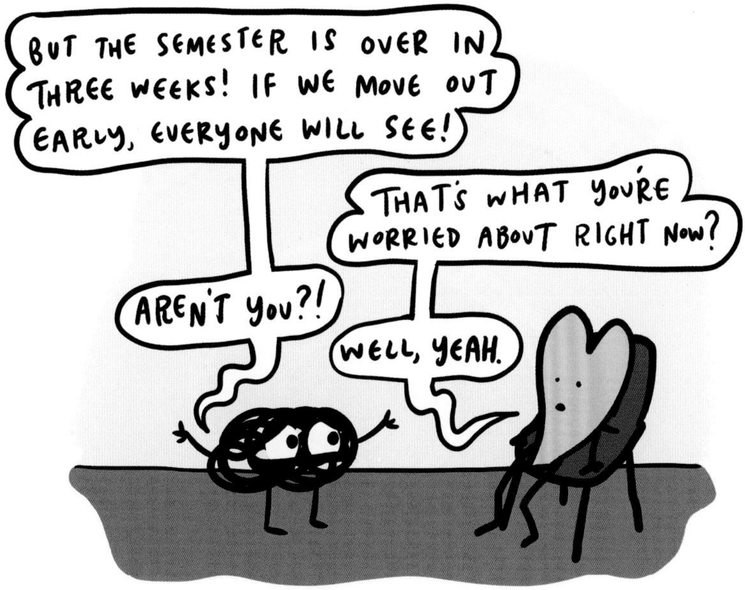
BUT THE SEMESTER IS OVER IN THREE WEEKS! IF WE MOVE OUT EARLY, EVERYONE WILL SEE!
THAT'S WHAT YOU'RE WORRIED ABOUT RIGHT NOW?
AREN'T YOU?!
WELL, YEAH.

I spent the rest of that meeting frantic, assuring the dean that these hospital visits were freak occurrences—after all, I'd made the dean's list last semester! I was student athlete of the week three separate times! I swore I would change, that I'd learned my lesson, cross my heart and hope to die.

After two days of deliberation, it was decided that I could finish the year out and even return next semester. My consequence instead would be weekly sessions with a notoriously out-of-touch counselor at the student health center. The school also used a points system to track students getting in trouble—reach ten, and you were expelled. After the second incident, I earned six, leaving little room for future mistakes. But both of these punishments paled in comparison to the shame that seemed to coat me like peanut butter, my thoughts globbed down in spirals of cruel self-talk.

I spent most of my time in my dorm, leaving only to go to class and the rooms of my two closest friends. Outside of that, venturing onto campus meant I could possibly run into someone I knew, someone who might give me a pitying glance or even worse: avert their eyes, pretending not to know me at all. My roommate and I existed in silence, a layer of unspoken awkwardness hovering like a thick mist between us after what had happened. Instead of studying for my upcoming exams, I scrolled Tumblr and rewatched episodes of *The Office*, taking comfort in familiar plots and dialogue and characters.

The weekends I used to look forward to were now the worst. I didn't crave the escape of a drink when I was alone, instead yearning for the social connection I felt when I drank with people. I wanted to see Anxiety flicker and fade into the background as the Partier lifted me onto his shoulders, helping me find my sense of belonging between sips. But instead I was curled under my comforter as the party music from neighboring dorm rooms made its way through the walls, a reminder that it all went on without me.

A few days before my parents would arrive to help me pack up my dorm and head back home, it seemed like summer had arrived a month early. The cycle of test taking and studying had blurred the last few days of the school year together, while my downtime was spent suffering in the stifling heat of my un-air-conditioned dorm room. My bed was damp with sweat where I'd been sitting, and even turning the box fan on my face provided little relief. I instinctively grabbed my phone to text my friends in hopes of getting an ice cream cone in town, but then remembered they'd both finished their finals and had moved out already. I hadn't seen the Partier in days, Anxiety acting as my sole (and loud) companion.

I sighed loudly, put a hat on, and went outside.

All I wanted was to follow him, to walk through the doors of that
house and feel like I wasn't a social pariah.

Even in the shade, the humidity felt heavy on my skin. Campus was pretty empty. I imagined most people were either following the Partier off campus for a backyard rager or sitting in the library, flipping through a study guide. I should've been there too—my Shakespeare paper needed a thorough edit—but instead, I pulled my knees up toward my chest, making myself as small as I could.

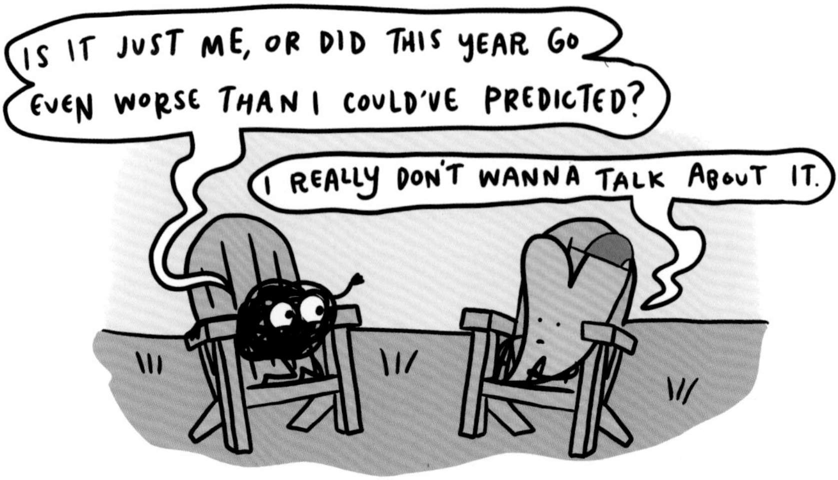
IS IT JUST ME, OR DID THIS YEAR GO EVEN WORSE THAN I COULD'VE PREDICTED?
I REALLY DON'T WANNA TALK ABOUT IT.

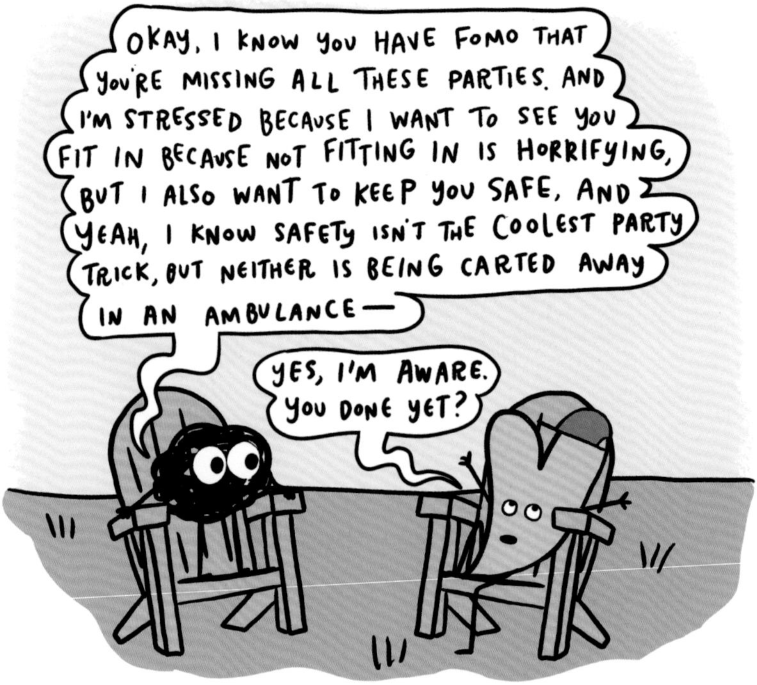
OKAY, I KNOW YOU HAVE FOMO THAT YOU'RE MISSING ALL THESE PARTIES. AND I'M STRESSED BECAUSE I WANT TO SEE YOU FIT IN BECAUSE NOT FITTING IN IS HORRIFYING, BUT I ALSO WANT TO KEEP YOU SAFE, AND YEAH, I KNOW SAFETY ISN'T THE COOLEST PARTY TRICK, BUT NEITHER IS BEING CARTED AWAY IN AN AMBULANCE—
YES, I'M AWARE. YOU DONE YET?

I rolled my eyes but nodded, squinting as a few students walked by with bagel sandwiches from the café.

I wouldn't know this for a while, but I was far from rock bottom. Come September, I would go back to school as a sophomore and pretend that the previous year hadn't happened. When people at parties would mention my trips to the hospital, I'd crack a beer and joke about how I'd been a stupid freshman. I would fall back into performing as the person I'd so desperately wanted to be, the one who saw the Partier's guidance as a magic trick that made Anxiety disappear with a poof. I would pledge to a sorority with a reputation for partying, a sorority I'd be in for only thirty days because yes, I'd go to the hospital again after a sister handed me a bottle of Moscato and told me to drink up, we were going *out*! I'd get suspended for two semesters, and no, not even that would be rock bottom.

That's because for years and years, even after returning to school as a junior and remaining sober until the final party of the year, where I fell off a guy's shoulders and hit my head on the wet cement of a frat basement, I would not learn.

Even after turning twenty-one while studying abroad and deciding that my status as a legal drinker must have meant I couldn't mess up anymore, only to black out and wake up in a stranger's apartment thirty miles outside the city, I would not learn.

Even after my best friends expressed deep concern when I threw up and fell asleep in one of their beds, thinking it was my own, I would not learn.

Even after I graduated and thought drinking was still the only way to connect with people, embarrassing myself time and time and time again, I would not learn.

There was no single rock bottom, but rather a dark trail I couldn't stop walking, truly believing a more lovable, funny, desirable me was somewhere in the shadows.

164

Of course I wasn't. But I nodded, closing my eyes and pressing my fingers onto my eyelids until I blocked out the sunlight entirely.

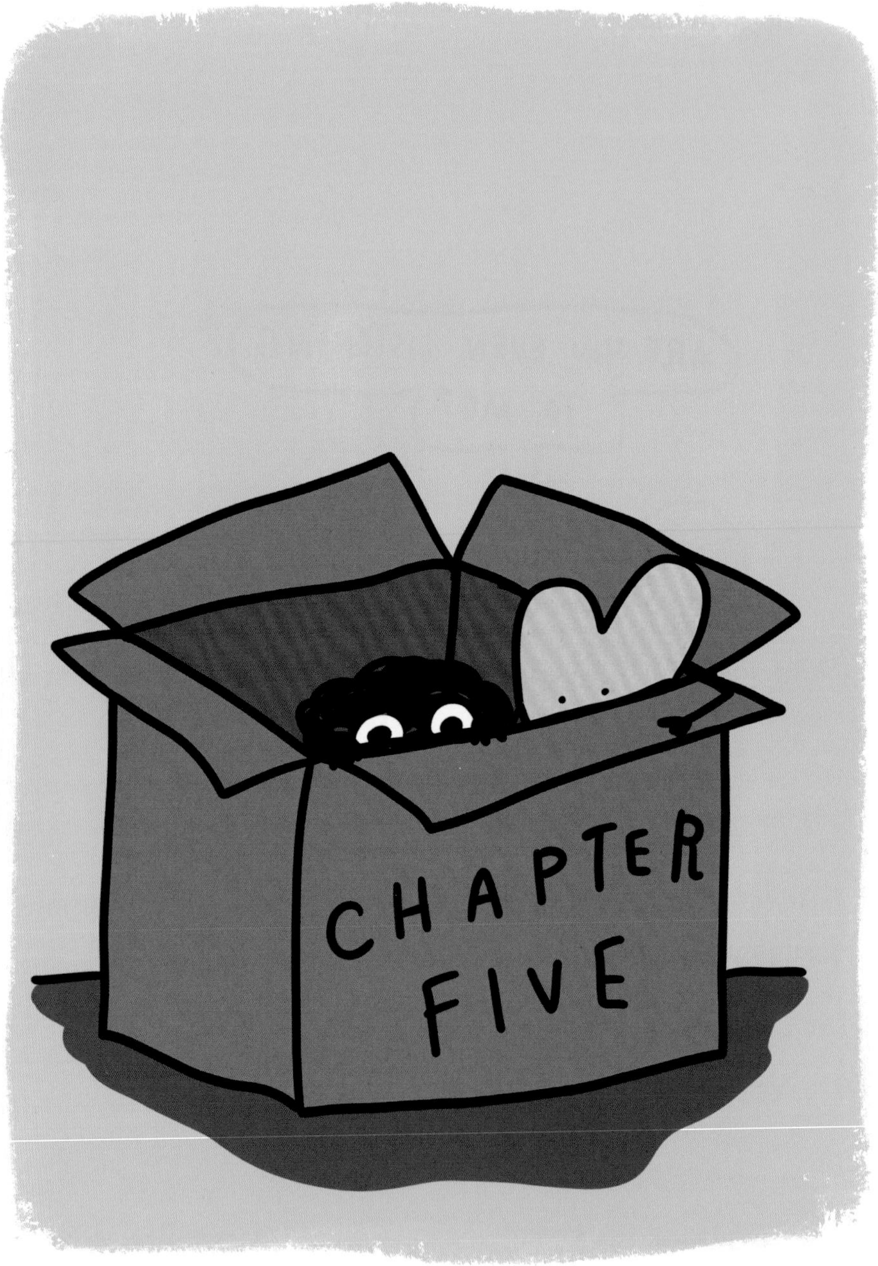
CHAPTER
FIVE

You wouldn't know it from the outside, but my first home in Seattle was a portal to the seventies.

Faded slats of wood paneled the walls of the basement, a strip of carpet had been glued to the top of the fireplace ledge, and heavy patterned curtains hung over each of the bedroom windows, surely left behind by the previous renters.

But the mirrors were weirdest of all—screwed into the walls of almost every hallway and room like a carnival funhouse. I kept making accidental eye contact with myself as I lugged my belongings from the car to my bedroom at the end of the hallway.

My reflection surprised me each time, as if I couldn't fully believe I was actually there, that I'd made it to Seattle.

My three roommates had moved in earlier that week, their belongings scattered around the house like Easter eggs: the bright book spines stacked under the coffee table, the framed posters propped against the wall, the half-full bottle of cheap red wine on the kitchen table, which we finished in the living room with my parents after the last of my things had been carried through the front door.

I drove my parents to the airport the next morning, where I hugged them tightly before watching them roll their suitcases through the sliding doors.

Thanks to the standstill traffic on I-5, the journey home became a prolonged tour of the city. White arches stretched like upside-down hammocks across the top of the football stadium, and the Space Needle's unmistakable silhouette seemed to puncture the gray sky. I saw tunnels covered in graffiti, boats floating on Lake Union, and green signs indicating exits for neighborhoods I had yet to visit.

But the most surprising sight of all was waiting for me in front of the house.

Indeed it was him, boxes and all.

There were loads of cardboard cubes in the back of the truck, varied in size and stacked in neat rows. And unfortunately, they all belonged to me.

I imagined my new roommates watching us parade the boxes into the house, piling them on the yellow kitchen counters or behind the couches or even in their bedrooms. I shook my head at the thought.

When I first learned about the Compartmentalizer from my elementary school counselor, I was unsure we'd get along.

And with that, she handed me a business card with an unfamiliar face and phone number printed across the front.

MEET THE COPING MECHANISM
THE COMPARTMENTALIZER

CAN PACK EVEN THE MOST INTRUSIVE THOUGHTS AND FEELINGS AWAY!

CALL 1-800-COMPART

I folded it in half and slipped it into the pocket of my jeans, forgetting about its existence the second I left her office to return to class. And I didn't think of it again for the rest of the day.

Well, not until I got in bed that night.

I stumbled out of bed toward my hamper, pulling my wrinkled jeans out from the mound of dirty clothes.

Anxiety watched from my bed as I dialed the number on my family's landline phone, which I'd snuck into my room from the kitchen.

He held to his word, walking through my door just moments later. A belt of tools hung around his waist, and he hugged a clipboard to his chest.

And with that, his sales pitch began.

Extra-strength tape? I was sold, signing the contract before he even moved to the next slide.

To my surprise, it was as easy as that.

Once the first box was sealed, it felt as if I'd Marie Kondo-ed my mind.

Sure, even the strongest cardboard wasn't enough to keep my thoughts trapped for good, but it was nice knowing they'd be out of sight for the time being.

As time went on, my collection of boxes slowly grew.

HOW DO PLANES STAY IN THE SKY (200...

WHAT IF MY PARENTS DISAPPEAR? (2000)

FOOTAGE OF THE TWIN TOWERS FALLING (2001)

WHEN MY DOG SPOT DIED (2001)

AM I A BAD BIG SISTER? (2002)

WHAT IF I'M UGLY? (20...

THE TIME I LIED AT ASHLEY'S PARTY (200...

WHAT HAPPENS AFTER WE DIE? (2003)

OH MY GOD CLIMATE CHANGE (2005-FOREVER)

WILL I EVER HAVE MY FIRST KISS? (2006)

WHY IS MY FRIEND AVOIDING ME? (2007)

WHEN MY COACH TOLD ME TO LOSE WEIGHT (2009)

BODY SHAME (2010)

2000      2005      2010

AWKWARD EYE CONTACT WITH GUY I KISSED LAST NIGHT (20...)

SHOULD I HAVE MORE ROMANTIC EXPERIENCE BEFORE COLLEGE? (2011)

WILL I ALWAYS FEEL THIS LONELY? (2013)

WHO AM I OUTSIDE OF SWIMMING? (2015)

WHAT IF I ANNOY MY FRIENDS? (2014)

TRIPPING IN FRONT OF TINDER DATE (2016)

GRANDPA'S DEATH (2016)

WHAT IF MY WORK PERFORMANCE REVIEW GOES POORLY? (2017)

WHAT IF I FAIL? (2017)

WHAT IF "THE BIG ONE" HAPPENS? (2017)

2011      2015      2017

But now, in the garage of my new house, I was in no mood to acknowledge the sheer volume of compartmentalized thoughts and
memories in storage. I had too much to do—a job to find! A dating
profile to update! Friends to make!

I recognized most of the boxes. After all, Anxiety had dusted them off and carried them to me over the years, tugging at the tape or pointing out holes that had formed in the corners.

2001:

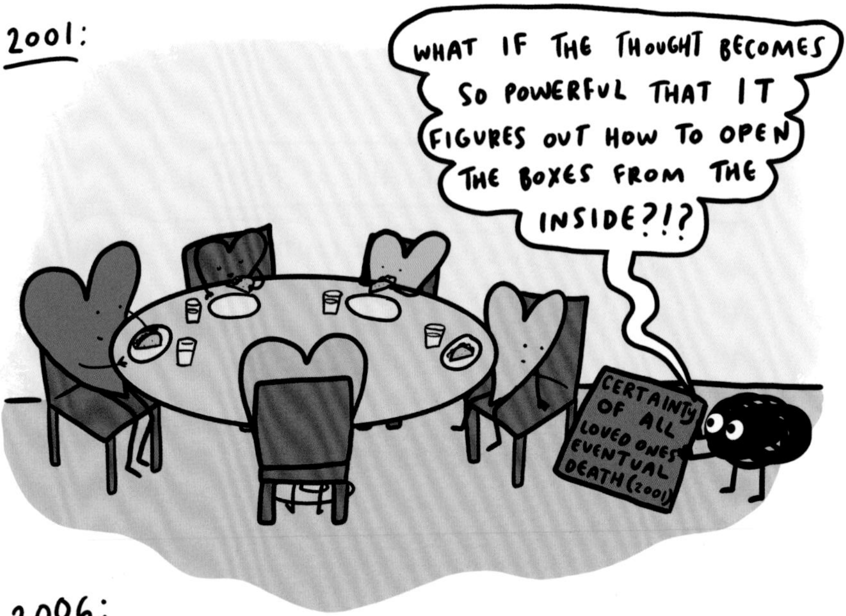
WHAT IF THE THOUGHT BECOMES SO POWERFUL THAT IT FIGURES OUT HOW TO OPEN THE BOXES FROM THE INSIDE?!?
CERTAINTY OF ALL LOVED ONES' EVENTUAL DEATH (2001)

2006:

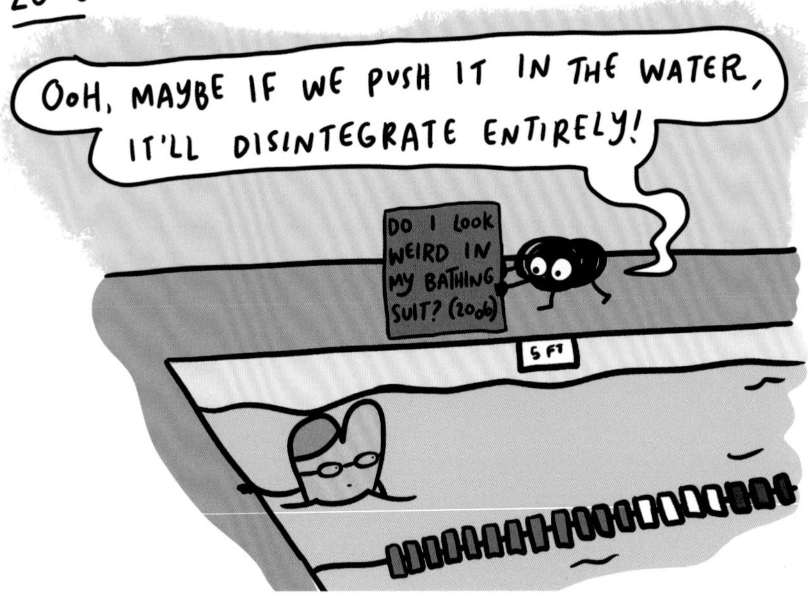
OoH, MAYBE IF WE PUSH IT IN THE WATER, IT'LL DISINTEGRATE ENTIRELY!
DO I LOOK WEIRD IN MY BATHING SUIT? (2006)
5 FT

Others, I'd completely forgotten about.

When one of my roommates called me into the house to help her hang a poster, I couldn't escape the garage quickly enough.

The rest of the day was full of distractions. We had furniture to arrange, dishes to stack in the cabinets, and books to organize by color on the shelves.

We ended the night in our new living room, planning a seventies-themed housewarming party while sipping beers.

When I finally collapsed on my mattress that night, my typical bedtime anxiety spiral was at odds with my post-move exhaustion.

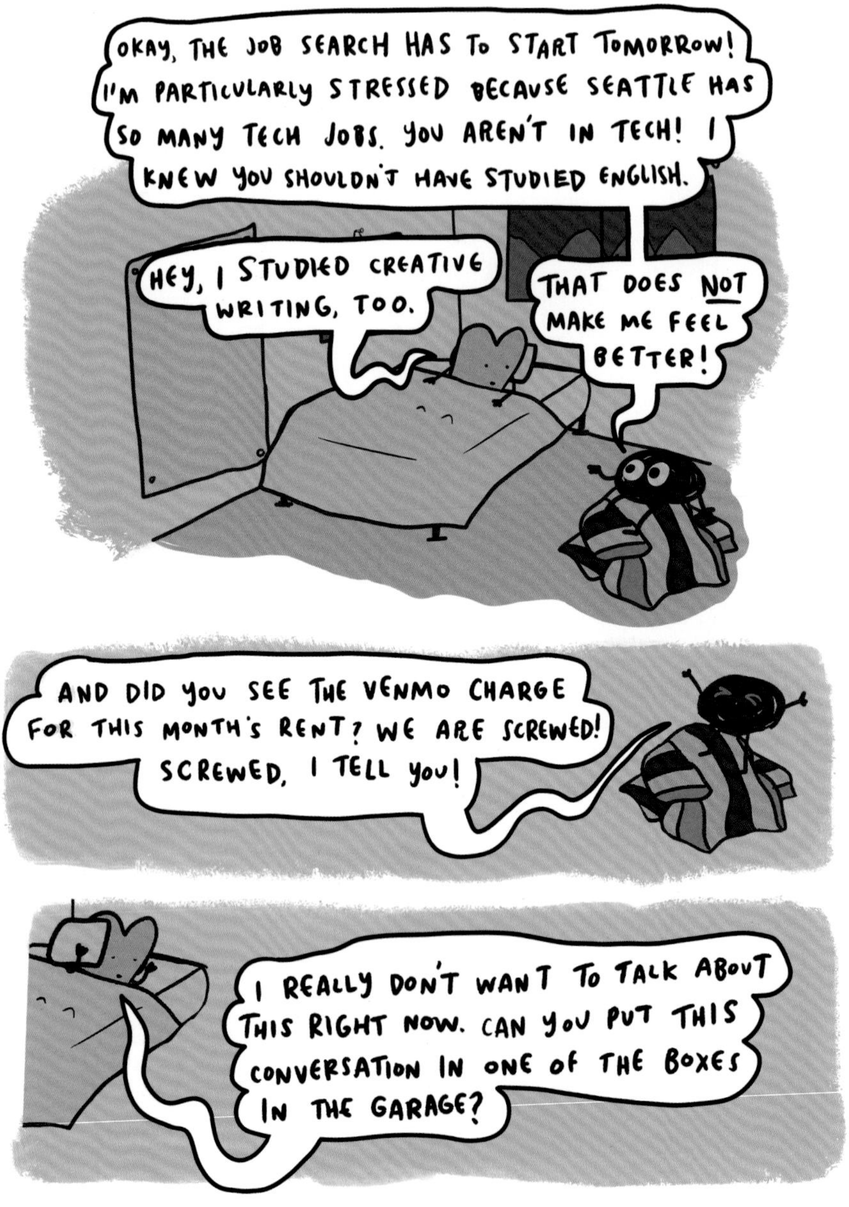
OKAY, THE JOB SEARCH HAS TO START TOMORROW! I'M PARTICULARLY STRESSED BECAUSE SEATTLE HAS SO MANY TECH JOBS. YOU AREN'T IN TECH! I KNEW YOU SHOULDN'T HAVE STUDIED ENGLISH.
HEY, I STUDIED CREATIVE WRITING, TOO.
THAT DOES NOT MAKE ME FEEL BETTER!
AND DID YOU SEE THE VENMO CHARGE FOR THIS MONTH'S RENT? WE ARE SCREWED! SCREWED, I TELL YOU!
I REALLY DON'T WANT TO TALK ABOUT THIS RIGHT NOW. CAN YOU PUT THIS CONVERSATION IN ONE OF THE BOXES IN THE GARAGE?

It was still dark outside when I woke up the next morning to a tapping sound.

But the noise repeated, and that's when I saw him, peering in through my window.

I sighed and got up, tiptoed down the hallway, and quietly opened the front door. But the boxes behind the Compartmentalizer weren't filled with anything. In fact, they weren't even boxes yet, still flat and stacked on top of each other like pancakes.

He dragged them past me and down the hall toward my room before I could protest further. I had no choice but to follow.

I guess it did count, because I watched as the Compartmentalizer packed and taped and labeled.

The sun was fully up by the time the Compartmentalizer was done.

I stood up, noticing some of the boxes had been placed in front of one of the mirrors screwed into the wall.

As we started to relocate them, I made eye contact with myself again. But this time, I didn't feel the glimmer of excitement I had yesterday while moving in.

The boxes. They multiplied in the mirror, and then again in the mirror on the opposite wall, an infinite sea of cardboard.

It hadn't felt like baggage in a long time, but that's exactly what it was, obstructing the rest of the world from sight. I was stuck with even the smallest worries I'd packed away, and there was nowhere to put them. But still, I decided I'd rather be in denial than face it head-on.

I ignored Anxiety's comment, instead stacking the new boxes like bricks in front of the mirrors.

I closed the door quietly as I left my room, scared that the boxes might topple over at even the slightest sound.

Control—the very thing I thought I had after deciding to leave everything behind in exchange for a new life. But I couldn't escape myself. The metaphorical baggage would show up at my step again and again.

So I kept my eyes on the ground as I walked down the mirrored hallway, avoiding my reflection as if I didn't exist at all.

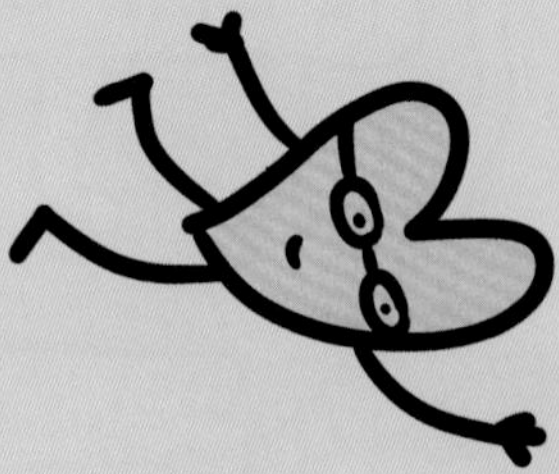

# CHAPTER SIX

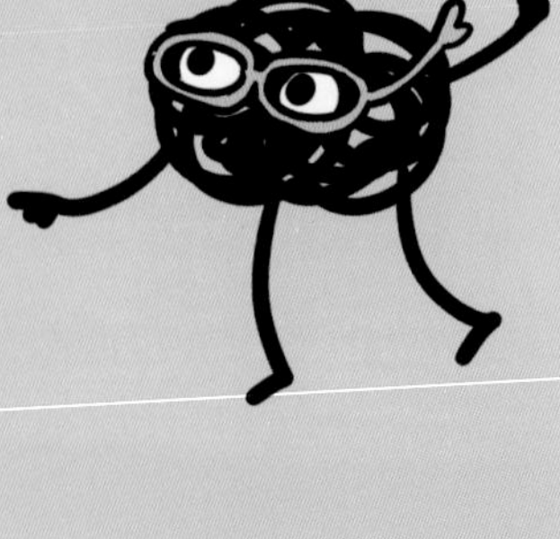

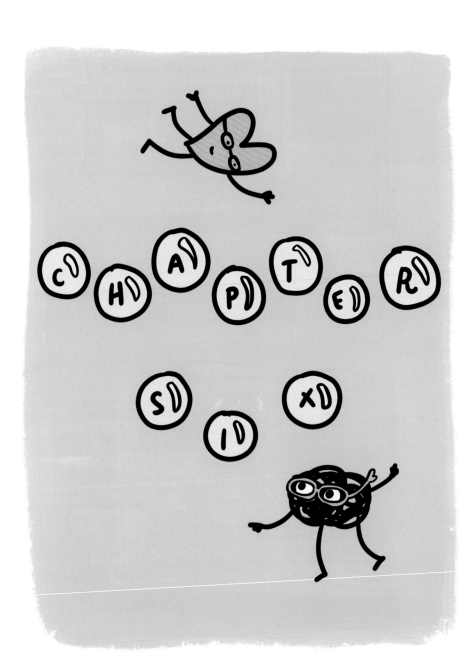

I wish I could say it was my destiny to be a swimmer.

But the truth is, I became a swimmer because I was terrible at everything else.

My almost comical lack of hand-eye coordination, coupled with the fact that both my parents grew up swimming competitively, led to my mom signing me up for the summer league swim team at our neighborhood pool.

Swim practice started midmorning. I'd line up with the other five-year-olds along the edge of the shallow end, goggles tightly strapped over our eyes. We took turns jumping in while holding our noses, and a teenage coach held my belly up as I kicked and flailed and pulled my head out of the water, gasping for air.

In a shocking twist of events, I *loved* it.

I loved how quiet it was beneath the surface, everything around me muted and muddled. I loved the swim meets, where I ate strawberry ice pops after finishing my single-lap races. I loved making up games in the deep end with my siblings, all of us jumping on my dad's back and begging to stay just a little longer.

And I loved that, no matter how hard he tried, Anxiety couldn't quite keep up with me.

That's because underwater, there was a different presence drawing me in. Some might call it endorphins. To me, she was the Diver.

The Diver loved the water even more than I did. She showed me how freeing it felt to jump off the diving board, to touch the tiles at the bottom of the pool, to float on the surface with our arms and legs splayed out like sea stars.

When my parents asked if I wanted to try out for a year-round swim team following my ninth birthday, I danced around the kitchen, thrilled that the end of summer would no longer mean the end of swimming.

A week later, I performed each of the four strokes in the shallow end of an Olympic-sized pool, showing off my best technique to the coach pacing the deck. My dad sat on the bleachers and gave me a thumbs-up when I finished.

The club team had over eight hundred kids divided into groups based first on age and then speed. I was assigned to the mid-tier group for nine- and ten-year-olds, but beyond that, I didn't know much about the place where I'd be spending four afternoons and one Saturday morning a week. Even still, I figured I would be a great addition to the team. Just two months ago I had been part of a record-breaking relay with my summer league team, as evidenced by the blue ribbon I'd pinned to my bedroom wall.

But when I walked through the entryway of the aquatic center on my first day of practice, I felt intimidated by the glass cases lining the walls. They were filled with trophies and championship plaques and photographs of swimmers on podiums, the medals around their necks catching the glint of the camera's flash. From every direction, it was clear this was a place where champions were made.

And then there was the pool.

It was the same fifty-meter pool I'd tried out in, but with various practice groups in session, it looked bigger and uninviting. The deck was a long expanse of wet concrete, and aside from the narrow windows along the walls, there wasn't much natural light reaching the water. But what felt most daunting were the bleachers bordering the pool, packed with kids who seemed like they knew they belonged there, stretching and straightening the straps of each other's bathing suits.

I perched myself on the edge of the first row as a tall man in a team-branded baseball cap walked onto the deck.

And that's when I learned what life as a year-round swimmer really looked like. My new coach described the coming year's schedule, noting the intersquad meets and the dual meets and the qualifier meets and the championship meets, all packed in before school let out for the summer. We were expected to attend every practice, and when he passed out sheets of paper that listed the race time standards he hoped we would each hit that year, I realized I was nervously chewing on the straps of my goggles.

The forty swimmers in my group were divided among six lanes, and though I felt awkward as I stood behind some girls laughing over an inside joke, the unease of being one of the new kids seemed to dissipate the moment I dove in. Sure, the water here was colder than my neighborhood pool, and the number of laps we were expected to swim was far more than I was used to, but the movements were the same.

It didn't take long, however, for practice to start kicking my ass.

The first few months on the team felt like I had accidentally signed up for a rigorous boot camp. We did more yardage in a week than I had in a month on my summer league team, and swimming was often followed by "dryland," a term attributed to the crunches and squats and pull-ups we'd do in a small room just off the aquatic center's entryway.

But at the same time, I found myself slowly making friends at both practice and the weekend-long swim meets. It was almost as if the chlorine was a platonic love spell, helping me bond with my teammates first over our shared sport and then everything else.

And with all this time spent in the pool came results. My technique slowly improved over the next few weeks and months, as did my endurance and speed.

Best of all, my worries still seemed to melt away during practice. It didn't matter where I sat at lunch at school or how much homework I had or if I got invited to the big party everyone was talking about. For an hour and a half, my only job was to move back and forth between the walls of the pool like a ping-pong ball.

Even during my earliest days as a swimmer, I preferred practice far more than competing. Sometimes I felt like I was missing a crucial piece of hardware that my peers seemed to have: the deep desire to race, to win. I would've picked the quiet, almost therapeutic repetition of lap swimming any day.

But competitive swimming didn't work like that. Instead, I slowly moved up through my team's program—first to the mid-tier group for eleven- and twelve-year-olds, then to the next level a few months before I started eighth grade. With each movement up the ladder, the expectations of us at practice and in competition only got bigger. For a while, this was fine. It was the first time I felt like I had settled into the rhythm of being good at something, at having a purpose.

By age thirteen, I'd slipped into a full-blown swimmer identity.

I wore my team T-shirts to school almost every day, announcing who I was just by taking off my jacket. The journals I kept were replaced with practice logs, where I'd meticulously track the yardage we did each day. I even changed my AIM screen name to ChlorineQueen624.

I took immense solace in having a word to encapsulate who I was. I was a swimmer. I swam. It felt as if I'd been playing a long game of Marco Polo with myself, eyes closed and arms outstretched as I waded through water, finally finding the *real* me. What could go wrong?

It was also around this time that I started to feel acutely aware of my body.

Puberty had descended upon me in my preteen years, a natural addage of weight and height and acne changing both my appearance and my perception of myself. I began hiding under my baggy swim team sweatshirts rather than wearing them proudly as an identifier, and I reapplied concealer a few times a day, smearing it across my forehead and down the bridge of my nose like a disguise.

The one place I felt like I couldn't truly hide was in my bathing suit.

The one-piece I'd once slid into without a second thought began to feel like a display case, highlighting all the parts of my body I carefully covered up the rest of the day. I resented how my suit left red imprints on my shoulders and hips like temporary tattoos and I often found myself tugging the fabric away from my abdomen, trying to keep the tight polyester from accentuating where my rib cage stopped and my stomach began. When I walked from the locker room onto the pool deck, I'd hug my equipment bag to my chest, a momentary censorship of the terrain beneath it.

Part of me knew this was a common feeling, that adolescents often grew to dislike parts (or all) of their bodies. Even though I continued to cover myself the second I could, wrapping a towel around my torso after races or sitting with my knees pulled tightly to my chest, I found relief in the thought that I wasn't alone.

I looked forward to diving in for practice, comforted by how the water's surface distorted everything beneath it. And I still loved how swimming made me feel—how powerful my body felt as it plowed through the water, how it sent endorphins through the very limbs I had frowned at in the mirror earlier that day, and especially how it offered an escape from the cruel voice in my head, my focus only on the next dive, the next breath, the next lap.

When my coach asked me to talk at the end of practice a few weeks after my fifteenth birthday, I had no clue what he wanted to discuss. I'd been performing pretty well in practice, and my attendance was nearly perfect.

My coach was a middle-aged man who wore T-shirts with baggy cargo shorts every day, tossing a tennis ball at the wall as he watched our mid-level fifteen-to-eighteen-year-old group follow the set he'd written on the whiteboard. He was known for his boisterous laugh and distance-heavy practices and coffee breath. I was desperate for his approval.

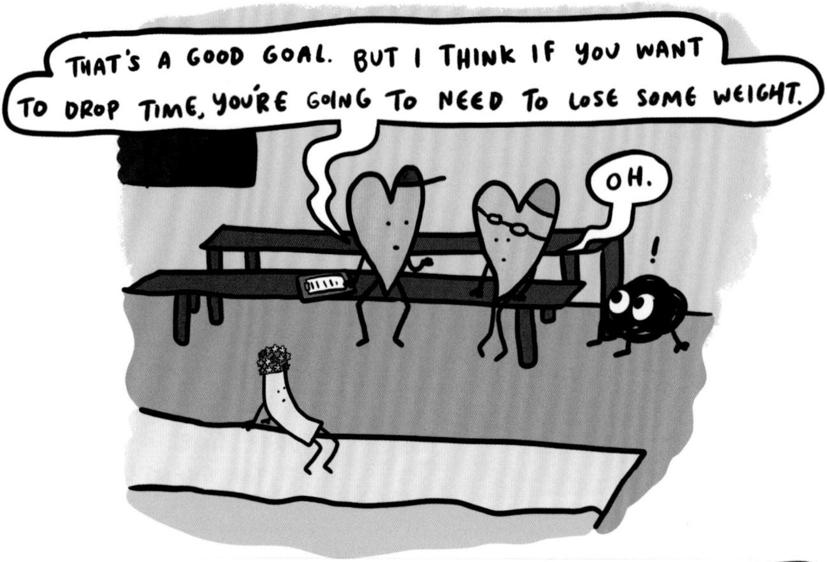
THAT'S A GOOD GOAL. BUT I THINK IF YOU WANT TO DROP TIME, YOU'RE GOING TO NEED TO LOSE SOME WEIGHT.
OH.
!

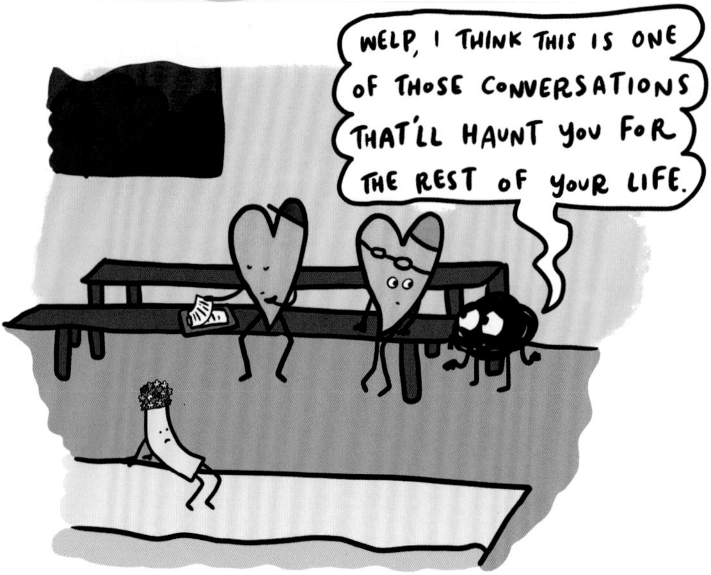
WELP, I THINK THIS IS ONE OF THOSE CONVERSATIONS THAT'LL HAUNT YOU FOR THE REST OF YOUR LIFE.

My coach nodded toward one of my teammates stretching farther down the deck, a friend of mine who was kind and shy and quite fast.

Lily and I were built quite differently. Where I had curves, Lily was lean and muscular. Where my thighs touched, hers did not. Where my suit hugged tight, hers hung a little loose. It felt as if she was a compact car and I was an SUV, looking on helplessly as a car salesperson tried to convince prospective buyers we were the same make and model.

I look back on this moment as an adult and feel sorry for Lily and sorry for me. No matter how little I ate or how often I held a plank, my body would never look like hers. But at the time, I just looked at my coach and nodded.

I didn't tell anyone about that conversation—for a while, my cheeks would flare red with shame whenever I thought about it. When I dove in the pool the next day at practice, I could hardly bear to look at the Diver.

And even worse: Anxiety was learning to swim.

I didn't lose weight. I don't even know what I would've done to try, since my training schedule already required more calories than I was consuming. But my discomfort with my appearance slowly morphed into self-loathing. My fear that my body was a problem had been confirmed, and it left me wishing I was a hermit crab, able to escape my current shell for a new one.

I found myself working harder in practice than I ever had before. The more I pushed myself, the harder it was to think about anything but the ache in my muscles, the burn in the back of my throat.

But it remained therapeutic, helping to unravel the mass of criticism knotting in my brain.

I guess the hard work paid off—I ended up having a great season-ending meet. In fact, I swam fast enough to move up to the top practice group in the coming season.

In the top group, however, I was at the bottom of the barrel. Many of my teammates had swum fast enough to go to national meets; some had even already qualified for the Olympic trials. I spent the two-hour practices worrying that the person leading my lane might lap me, and secretly wished I could think of an excuse to get out of practice.

Worst of all, Anxiety and the Diver were at odds the whole time.

The only saving grace of this group was my friends. Since there were seven practices during the week, most of my time was spent with them either in the pool or at a café nearby, recounting the horrors of the previous practice while stealing bites of hashbrowns from each other's plates.

But I couldn't help comparing myself to them. I was the slowest of my friend group, and as college recruitment became a topic of conversation, I felt like an imposter, a blinking satellite in a sky of shooting stars.

I never thought to ask myself why I wanted to swim in college, instead accepting it as the next step in competitive swimming—and my life.

My performance at swim meets had tanked since moving up to the top group. Even though I had once seen competition as just another part of swimming, the seriousness my coach placed upon each race left a buzz of panic in my chest.

It got to the point that I'd tremble behind the block before a race, nausea claiming my stomach.

I sobbed on the drive home from almost every swim meet. My parents sat in the front seat, unsure of how to console me. I guess that's why we ended up at my doctor's office halfway through my junior year of high school.

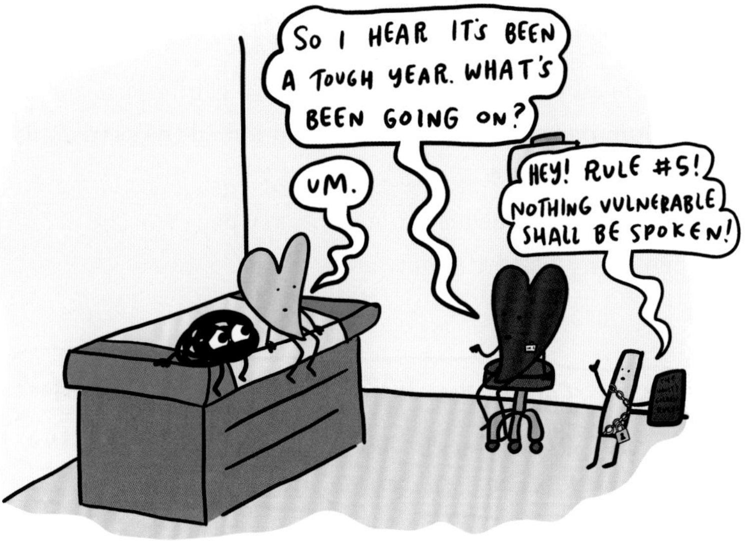
SO I HEAR IT'S BEEN A TOUGH YEAR. WHAT'S BEEN GOING ON?
UM.
HEY! RULE #5! NOTHING VULNERABLE SHALL BE SPOKEN!

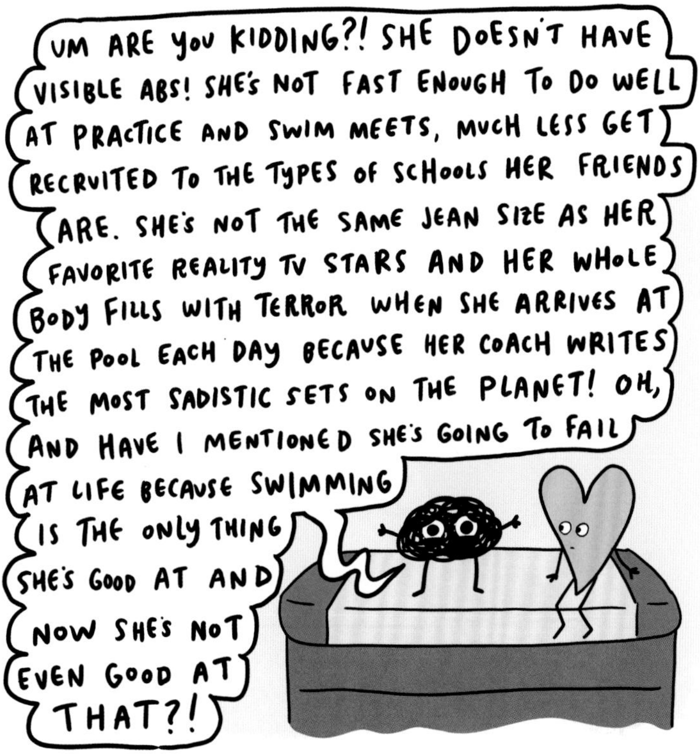
UM ARE YOU KIDDING?! SHE DOESN'T HAVE VISIBLE ABS! SHE'S NOT FAST ENOUGH TO DO WELL AT PRACTICE AND SWIM MEETS, MUCH LESS GET RECRUITED TO THE TYPES OF SCHOOLS HER FRIENDS ARE. SHE'S NOT THE SAME JEAN SIZE AS HER FAVORITE REALITY TV STARS AND HER WHOLE BODY FILLS WITH TERROR WHEN SHE ARRIVES AT THE POOL EACH DAY BECAUSE HER COACH WRITES THE MOST SADISTIC SETS ON THE PLANET! OH, AND HAVE I MENTIONED SHE'S GOING TO FAIL AT LIFE BECAUSE SWIMMING IS THE ONLY THING SHE'S GOOD AT AND NOW SHE'S NOT EVEN GOOD AT THAT?!

I wish I could've admitted the extent of it, that I wasn't just feeling weird, but rather as if a permanent knot was forming in my stomach. I wish I could have said that I fantasized about spraining my ankle or getting a head cold—anything to ensure I'd miss a few practices. I wish I could have told her how much I pinched the skin on my stomach and legs, willing it to go away.

But instead, I forced a smile, the waxy paper on the examination table crinkling as I shifted my legs.

My cheeks felt hot. Of course I was going to keep swimming, I wanted to say. Who was I without it? I tried to imagine my afternoons after school, empty with no practice to attend. The uncertainty of a life without it felt ten times scarier than soldiering on in the pool.

The appointment ended with my doctor saying I was physically healthy, but that it sounded like I was experiencing sports performance anxiety. She prescribed me an antianxiety medication, hoping it would help mitigate the unhelpful thoughts.

In a perfect world, this daily pill would do it all: turn my swimming career around, build a metaphorical dam around my insecurities, and even restore my love for the sport.

But the one I'd been prescribed was a bad fit for me.

My stress was slowly replaced with a fog of apathy. Instead of crying after a bad race, I just shrugged. Perhaps this was a welcome change from the flood of emotions I had become accustomed to, but I was actually swimming slower. A lot slower.

I didn't stay on it very long.

This was my first lesson in medication: It wasn't an immediate solution. Rather, it was a journey, one that would feel frustrating at times. I'd end up going on and off antidepressants well into my adulthood, eventually finding comfort in how they helped stabilize me.

But at the time, I wasn't willing to risk another poor pharmaceutical matchup. Not with so much on the line. I needed to go fast. I needed to be recruited for college. The way I saw it, there was no other path forward. Swimming felt much more important than my mental health.

Sometimes I wonder how it happened—how I made it through the final year of club swimming, how I continued to treat swimming like the pinnacle of my existence even when our relationship had clearly grown toxic.

I committed to swim for a division three program at a small liberal arts college. Fortunately, things took a turn for the better on my new team: the program was less intense, my teammates were fun, and best of all, I looked forward to swim practice again, even with the insecurity and race anxiety that had followed me there.

It also helped that my college swim coach seemed to recognize my anxiety early on, sitting me down in his office after our first meet to remind me that swimming, even competitively, was nothing more than a sport.

But it seemed that the self-doubt and the nausea twisting through my stomach before a race had seeped into my love for the sport like poison until it was impossible to separate the two. Anxiety had found his place in swimming, and I couldn't imagine the sport without his voice-over.

When I hung up my suit after my championship meet senior year, I had no intention of putting it back on again.

As a swimmer, I had spent a lot of time thinking about the end—the end of the practice, the end of the race, the end of the season—but I rarely thought about what would happen at the end of my swimming career.

The identity crisis began almost immediately.

I felt unsure of who I was without the militant structure of a practice schedule but tried to convince myself that it was a good thing. I was moving on. At least, that's what I told myself when I declined my dad's invitation to join him for a morning swim or a friend's request to spend a summer day by the pool. It was as if the search for myself started over.

I figured the answer had to be somewhere, so I looked for clues everywhere. At my first desk job:

And at the cycling classes I took with my mom:

And on the dance floors of crowded bars on late Friday nights:

I even moved across the country, hoping I'd find the answers there.

Here is what I wish I could have told myself: You're not going to find yourself in one place. Your true self wasn't waiting for you in the pool, and she isn't tapping her fingernails at the desk of your dream job. She's not sitting in another state or country, living the life you were always supposed to live.

Not unlike the water itself, you aren't static. Instead, you move with the waves of change and growth and setbacks. There is not one answer to the question "Who are you?" The answers could be infinite. The answers are never set.

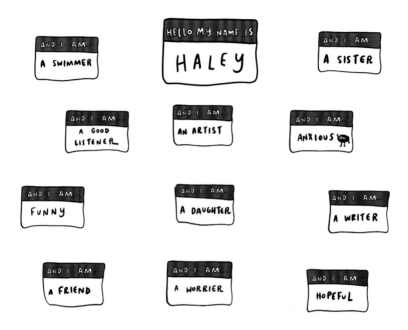

But that's not how lessons are learned.

One year after moving to Seattle, I spent a Sunday afternoon walking around a neighborhood near my house. Life was okay—I'd had two different jobs since moving out there, and for the first time in my life, I'd built a community that had nothing to do with swimming. But shocker: Anxiety was ever present, following me as I walked along the main drag.

I was thinking about grabbing a coffee when I noticed it—the scent of chlorine, thick and musty and unmistakable. I looked up and saw a massive neon sign in the shape of a woman diving above the name of a gym in bold yellow text. Without hesitating, I turned on my heel and walked through the door.

I followed her down the hall, where she opened a door and there it was: a small pool, divided into six lap lanes. Among the people swimming was a familiar face.

For the first time in a long time, the sight of it all—the Diver, the water, the lane lines and kickboards and pace clocks, even the thought of sliding my body back into a bathing suit—hit me like a wave of nostalgia rather than dread.

I came back the next day with my old practice suit and goggles in tow.

After just a few laps, my muscles felt like Jell-O, and I got water up my nose. But I felt as if I had found a reset button, one that brought me back to the feeling I'd had at the neighborhood pool all those years ago, where each splash and kick and breath felt new and strange and powerful.

I only swam for twenty minutes that day. After pulling the swim cap off my head, I leaned back until I was floating, my body supported by nothing but the water.

I'd never thought of it that way, that perhaps it could be the first time more than once.

I shook my head, finding comfort in the sudden realization that swimming didn't need to be the center of my life in order for me to return to it.

It could still be a part of me, though.

I could always begin again.

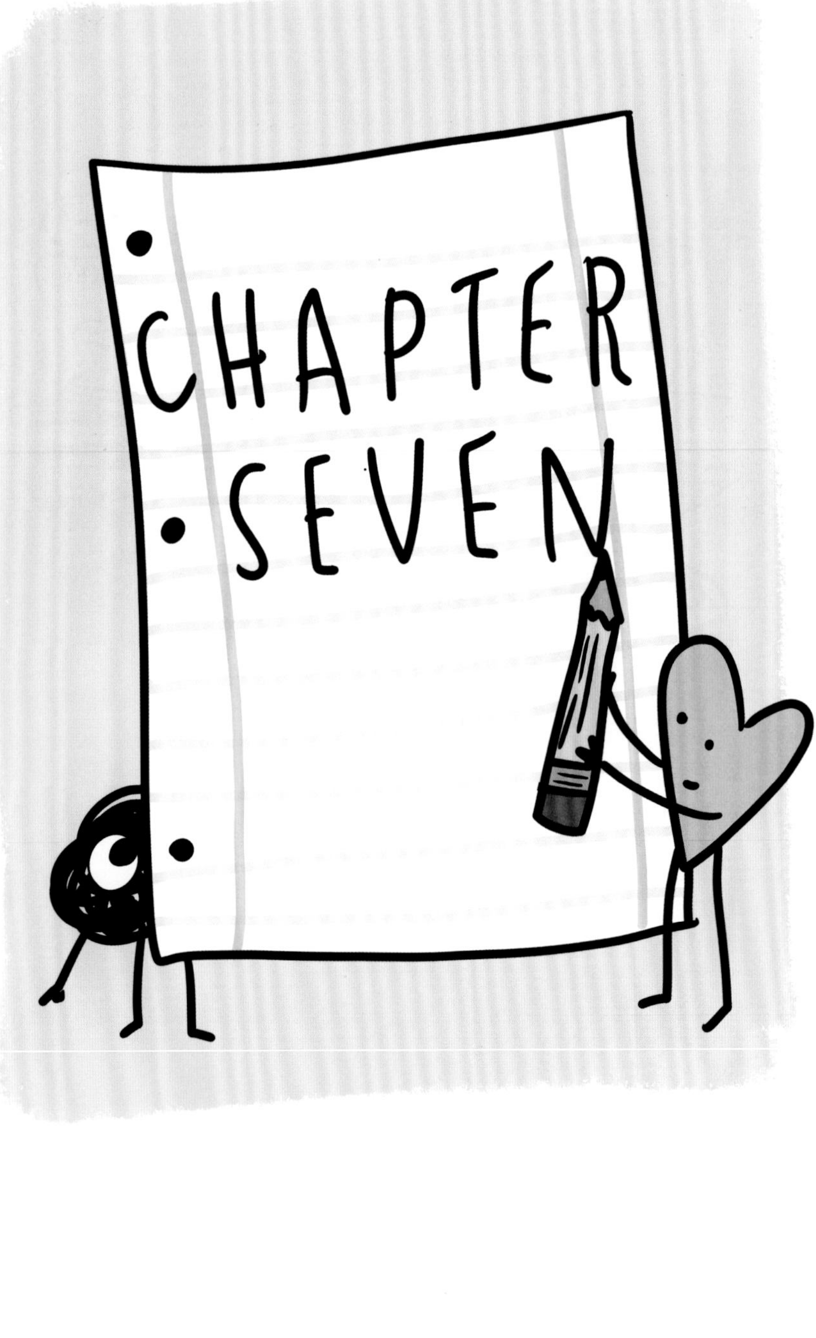
CHAPTER
SEVEN

When my parents moved out of my childhood home the year after I graduated college, my mom called to ask me what I wanted to do with my journals.

The notebooks were waiting for me in a plastic storage bin on the floor of my old bedroom. I felt as if I stood before a ghost, and in a way, I did—each journal held thoughts I'd deemed important or painful or revelatory enough to be written down over the years. Needless to say, I was expecting to be wowed by even my earliest entries. Surely my tortured yet brilliant soul had been preserved in the pages!

When I opened my first-grade diary, however, I realized that perhaps I hadn't been the emotional prodigy I'd thought I was.

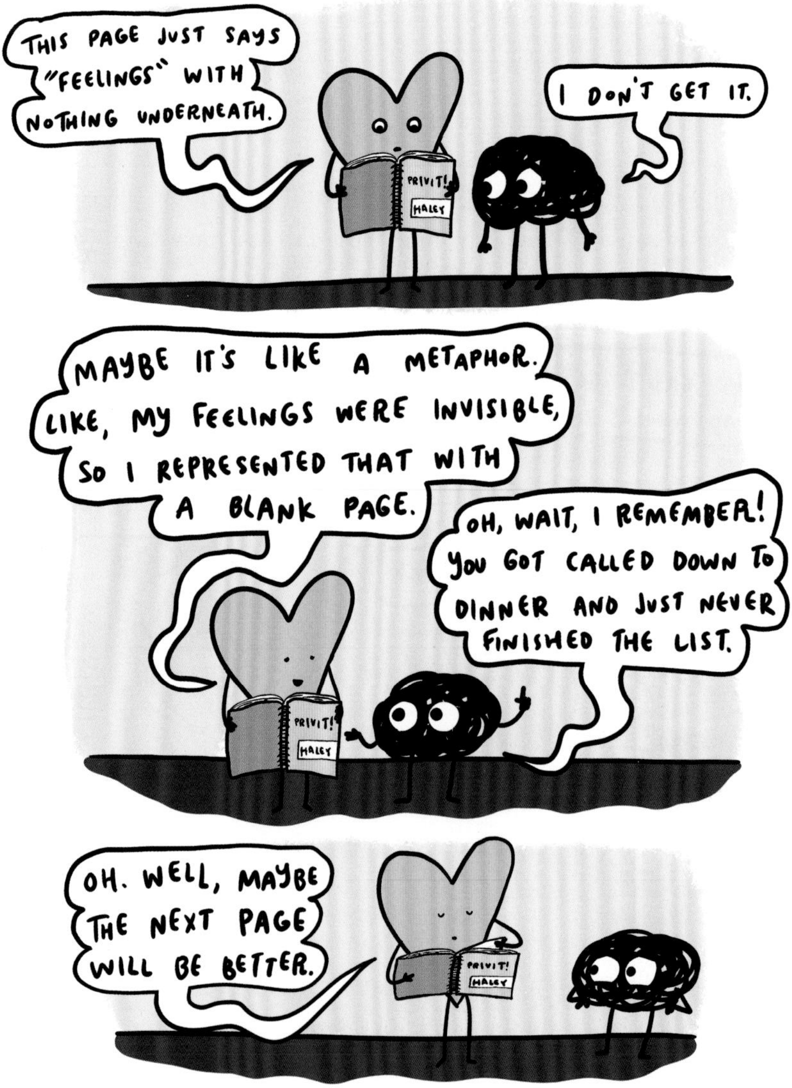
THIS PAGE JUST SAYS "FEELINGS" WITH NOTHING UNDERNEATH.
I DON'T GET IT.
MAYBE IT'S LIKE A METAPHOR. LIKE, MY FEELINGS WERE INVISIBLE, SO I REPRESENTED THAT WITH A BLANK PAGE.
PRIVIT!
HALEY
OH, WAIT, I REMEMBER! YOU GOT CALLED DOWN TO DINNER AND JUST NEVER FINISHED THE LIST.
OH. WELL, MAYBE THE NEXT PAGE WILL BE BETTER.

It wasn't.

It was no secret that Anxiety preferred the Writer to most of my other coping mechanisms.

MEET THE COPING MECHANISM

# THE WRITER

## KNOWN FOR

- HAVING THE BEST PEN COLLECTION
- SENDING THE OCCASIONAL HEART-FELT CARD
- FINDING MEANING IN CHAOS

Not unlike a massage therapist, the Writer helped stretch Anxiety out, loosening his tangly body with each word and doodle written across the page.

But loosen what exactly, I certainly couldn't tell as I continued to leaf through my notebooks.

As I got older, the entries seemed to fall into one of two camps.

CAMP ONE: SAD ☹

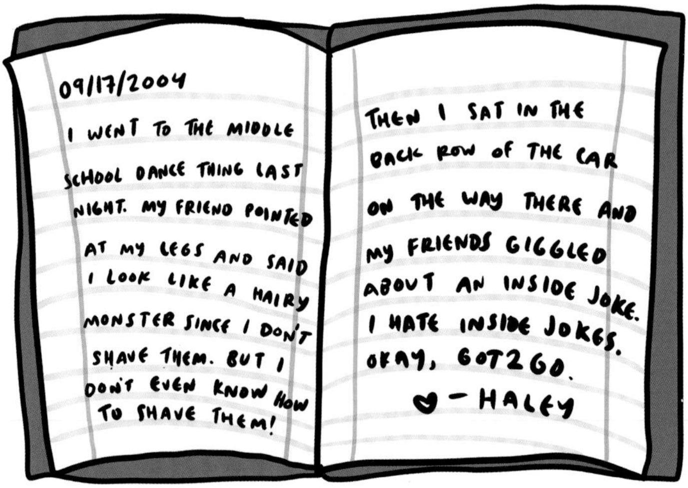
09/17/2004
I WENT TO THE MIDDLE SCHOOL DANCE THING LAST NIGHT. MY FRIEND POINTED AT MY LEGS AND SAID I LOOK LIKE A HAIRY MONSTER SINCE I DON'T SHAVE THEM. BUT I DON'T EVEN KNOW HOW TO SHAVE THEM!
THEN I SAT IN THE BACK ROW OF THE CAR ON THE WAY THERE AND MY FRIENDS GIGGLED ABOUT AN INSIDE JOKE. I HATE INSIDE JOKES. OKAY, GOT2GO.
♥ -HALEY

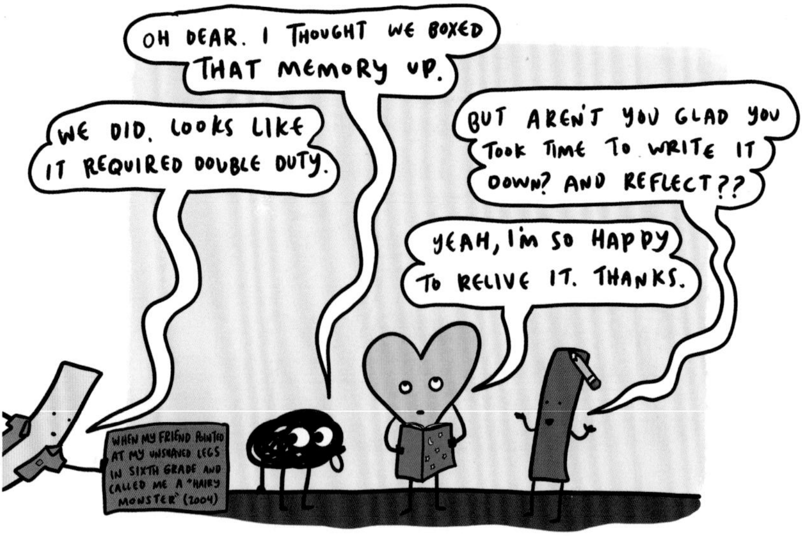
OH DEAR. I THOUGHT WE BOXED THAT MEMORY UP.
WE DID. LOOKS LIKE IT REQUIRED DOUBLE DUTY.
BUT AREN'T YOU GLAD YOU TOOK TIME TO WRITE IT DOWN? AND REFLECT??
YEAH, I'M SO HAPPY TO RELIVE IT. THANKS.
WHEN MY FRIEND POINTED AT MY UNSHAVED LEGS IN SIXTH GRADE AND CALLED ME A "HAIRY MONSTER" (2004)

# CAMP TWO: SAD  BUT ALSO INFORMATIVE!

As I continued searching my own words for hidden meaning or insight, I only found myself growing more disappointed.

But then we found something else.

My younger sister, Charlotte, and I drew a lot when we were little. Mom would set markers and crayons and a whole ream of computer paper on the kitchen table, transforming the dining nook into a temporary art studio. We doodled everything: dogs, our dream houses, cool girls in tube tops and flared jeans, even cruise ships designed brightly from bow to stern.

We stopped doing it as much when I started middle school, my embarrassment about pretending overtaking the joy of creating.

I'd been a little out of practice with all forms of creativity lately, turning to it only when I felt "inspired" (which was never). At least, this was the case when the Writer showed up that evening with a sketchbook tucked under her arm.

I only drew things I knew how to draw: flowers and disproportionate faces and uneven stars. Squiggles and hearts and my name in block letters. The superman *S*. Circles, triangles, staircases leading nowhere. But I had to admit even the simplest lines felt nice, like a release.

Maybe I didn't have to be an emotional prodigy or craft the perfect paragraph or even draw a masterpiece.

Giving my feelings a more recognizable shape was enough. It always had been—it just took a moment to remember.

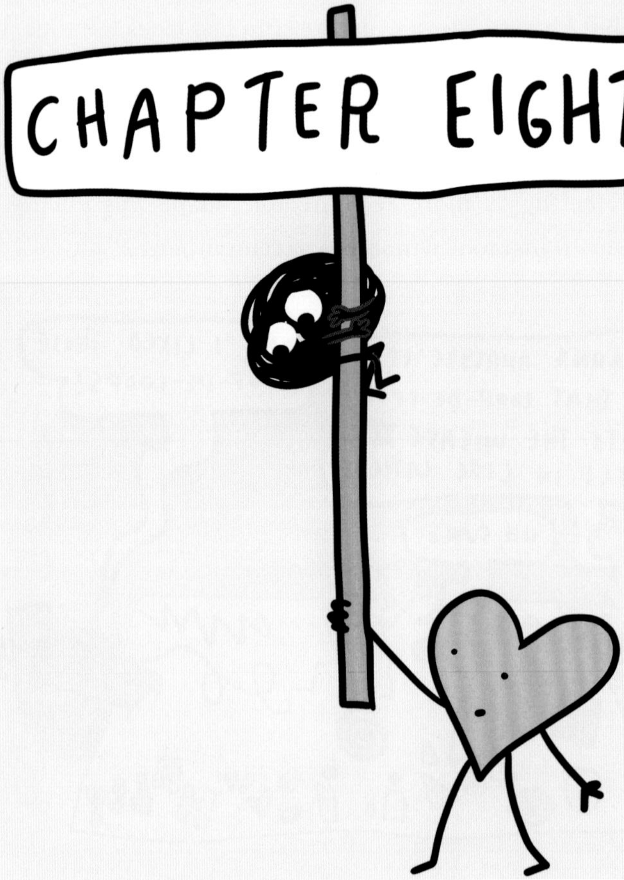
CHAPTER EIGHT

There's no better escape than being someplace new.

At least, that's how I felt during my first few months living in Seattle. Even with the Compartmentalizer's recent drop-off, I busied myself to the point that there was no time to acknowledge the boxes lining the walls of my bedroom and the garage. My days were spent downtown at the underpaying nine-to-five I'd secured a few weeks into my job search, and when I arrived back home in the evenings, at least one of my roommates was around and ready to do something: go to a concert, drink beers on the grassy hill overlooking Lake Union, gossip on the back porch.

I was exhausted by the time I fell into bed each night, dozing off before the usual parade of anxious thoughts could march through.

So yes, being somewhere new was proving to be a fantastic temporary high.

But that's the thing: it's temporary.

Temporary, like summertime in the Pacific Northwest. Having arrived at the tail end of August, I was mesmerized by how long the sun hung like an ornament in the sky each day. The city seemed to glow with happiness under the thirteen-hour sweep of daylight—I wouldn't have been surprised if the people walking by burst into song.

The change was barely noticeable at first. Darkness crept in like a fog, slowly engulfing the light at the start and end of each day. And with the sunlight went my temporary high, the unfamiliar city and job and outings becoming what any big change eventually becomes: a new normal. It felt as if I'd taken off a pair of tinted glasses, the world in front of me no longer accentuated in bright hues.

And when Anxiety managed to hold my attention for a beat too long, I knew just who to call.

In hindsight, I was suffering from seasonal depression. But even as the dull sadness grew around me like thick weeds in a garden, I sidestepped the tangly leaves and roots as if I didn't notice them at all. And for a while, that worked.

At least, it worked until the night it happened.

It was a rainy Saturday night in January, and a few friends and I had just arrived at a new bar in a trendy neighborhood close to the city. I felt good—the beer I'd sipped right before seemed to part through the clouds in my brain like sunlight.

But that sunlight didn't last long. Instead, the rest of the night clouded in a haze: me talking to a friend, me excusing myself to go to the bathroom, me reapplying lipstick in the mirror, me returning to the dance floor, the music so loud and the crowd so dense I could barely move, me putting my drink on the bar (just for a moment!), another song, me remembering my drink, grabbing it, taking a small sip, me searching for familiar faces in the crowd, me spinning, the world twirling right alongside me.

And then, nothing. Nothing for the rest of the night. Nothing until I woke up the next morning, freezing. Nothing until, eyes still closed, I felt around for a blanket. Nothing until my hand landed on cold leather and my eyes opened to the ceiling of a car.

I was stretched across the back seat, still in my black jeans and coat from the night before. But I wasn't focused on my outfit, or on the stale scent lingering around me. This wasn't my car. I had no idea where I was.

I ignored him, stuffing my hands in my coat pockets and sighing with relief at the feeling of my phone and keys stowed inside.

I pushed the car door open and nearly fell out onto the street.

And I meant it. My ride arrived minutes later, and I got in without looking back.

I spent the drive home playing mind games with myself: counting backward from one hundred by threes, alphabetically listing animals, then foods, then names, even biting the insides of my cheeks to the beat of the song coming from the speakers.

When I finally stumbled through the front door of my house, I walked straight down the hall, past the mirrors screwed into the walls, past the closed doors of my probably sleeping roommates, and into my room, pushing boxes out of the way until I collapsed in my bed.

And with that, he turned on his heel and left.

Anxiety's voice was growing louder, his body twitching and en-larging with each vocalized worry.

It felt like a heavy rock had been placed on my chest. I couldn't speak. Or breathe. Or move. For a moment, I wondered if I was dying. All I could see was Anxiety ripping through the room, picking up the boxed-up thoughts and feelings and throwing them to the ground.

I don't know how long it lasted. The panicked feeling faded away slowly, like air leaking out of a balloon until it lay flat and deflated on the ground.

The rest of the day was a wash. I slept for most of it, exhaustion falling upon me as if I had just run uphill for miles. It wasn't until that evening that I woke up hungry, only to find Anxiety sitting at the edge of my bed like a crumpled ball of paper.

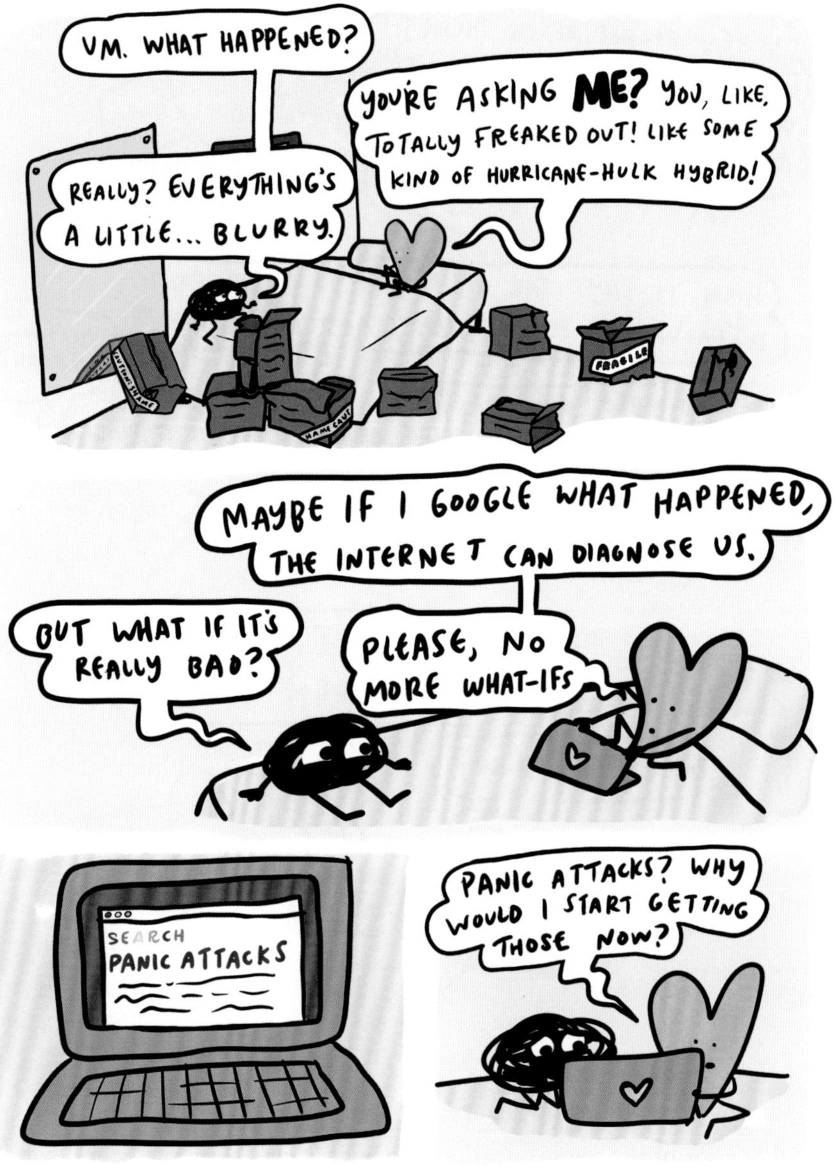
UM. WHAT HAPPENED?
YOU'RE ASKING ME? YOU, LIKE, TOTALLY FREAKED OUT! LIKE SOME KIND OF HURRICANE-HULK HYBRID!
REALLY? EVERYTHING'S A LITTLE... BLURRY.
FRAGILE
MAYBE IF I GOOGLE WHAT HAPPENED, THE INTERNET CAN DIAGNOSE US.
BUT WHAT IF IT'S REALLY BAD?
PLEASE, NO MORE WHAT-IFS
SEARCH
PANIC ATTACKS
PANIC ATTACKS? WHY WOULD I START GETTING THOSE NOW?

I looked at my room, overwhelmed by the number of boxes that had been toppled over. Surely this was a freak accident, a temporary low at the other end of my temporary high.

I guess I was determined to learn the hard way.

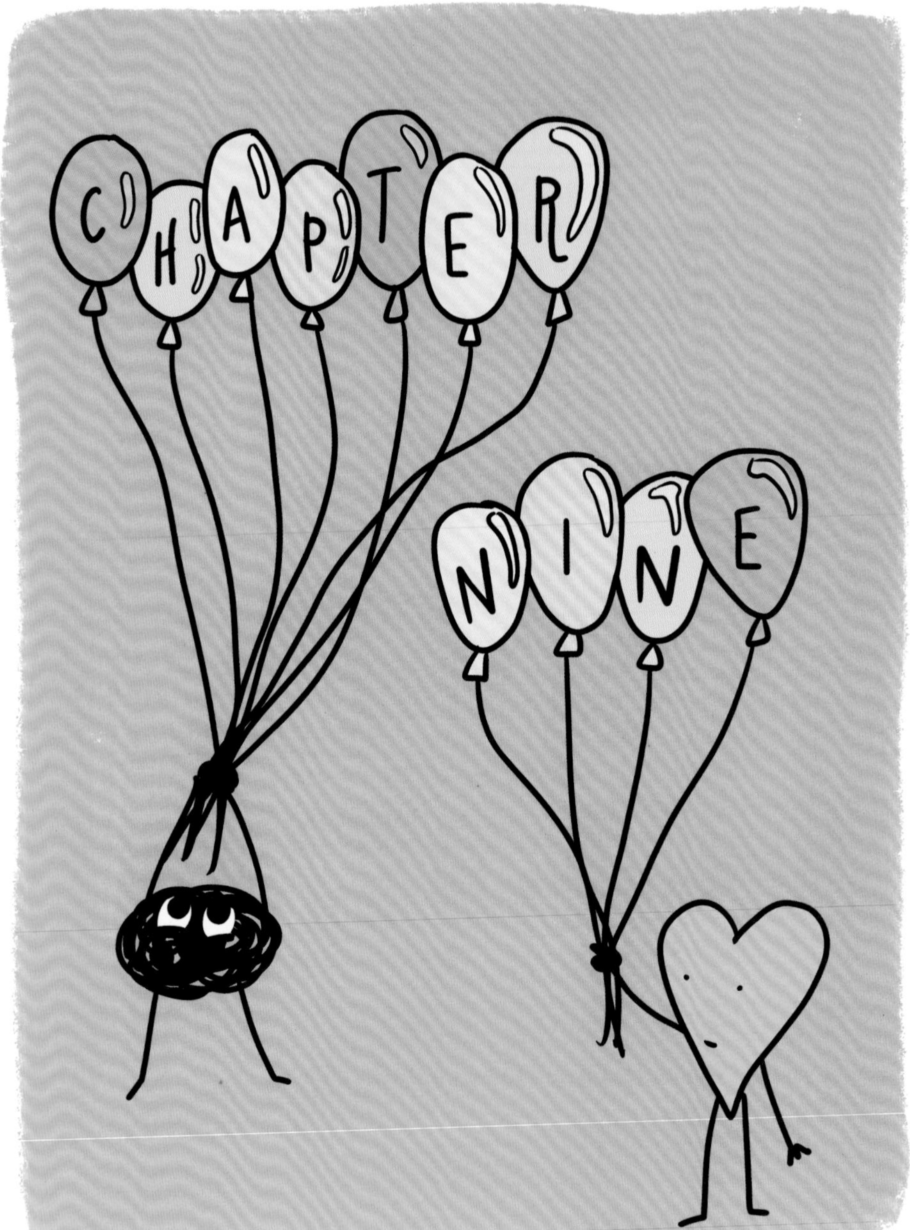
CHAPTER
NINE

I knew things were not going well when I realized my younger brother had become my therapist.

Well, kind of. At the time, talking to Graham was as close as I got to revealing the truth about my declining mental health. But I never admitted it outright. Instead, I circled my real feelings like a vulture over roadkill.

It had been six months since my first panic attack, and I had naively hoped it had been a one-time thing.

Instead, my panic attacks had no schedule, no promised arrival time. I felt like I was trapped in a horror movie, the kind where the jump scare makes your stomach drop and fast-forwarding to the credits feels like the only escape. Except this was real life. There was no fast-forward button. They showed up when they showed up, an airplane gone rogue. Sometimes a stressful work email was enough to trigger it. Another time, it arrived on a crowded dance floor, the wall of people almost impossible to get through. But more than anything else, my panic attacks thrived in the quiet darkness of my bedroom at night.

Not even the help of my coping mechanisms could defeat it.

The panic attack always stopped eventually, like a gust of wind dissipating into thin air. But instead of processing it, I was just happy it was over. And rather than talk to someone—even my brother—about what was happening, I begged the Compartmentalizer to help me find space to box it all away.

It went on like this through the rest of my first year living in Seattle. And if I wasn't dancing around my feelings on phone calls with Graham, I was flat-out avoiding them from behind a wall of distractions.

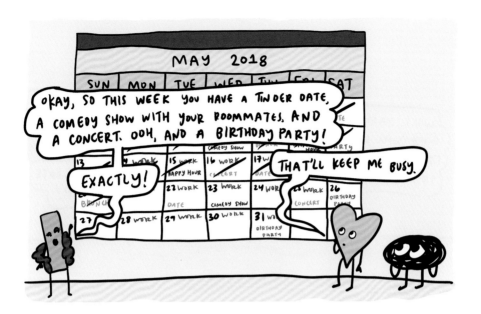

But the best distraction of all came along one day in June. My roommate Sam and I were swiping through dating apps when I came across his profile. He was handsome. Two years older than me. In grad school. Holding a baby goat in his picture. The Distractor nodded eagerly as I swiped right.

We met up the following week at a bar, only to realize we both loved the same bakery a neighborhood over. We shared a slice of chocolate cake by the Fremont Cut and a first kiss while playing a game of Jenga at a nearby arcade.

I fell hard, and I fell hard *fast*.

Oh, and I was absolutely terrified of scaring him off.

I felt like a Russian doll, stacking better versions around myself to hide what was at my core. I justified it to myself as protection for me and for him: if he couldn't see what stirred beneath the surface, we'd both win.

For a while, the excitement of being in a new relationship was all-consuming, acting as a repellent for my regularly scheduled worries.

But slowly, anxious thoughts found their way through the mist. I should have known they could bite at any time.

I liked sleeping at Gideon's apartment. Perhaps it was the way his arms wrapped around me as we slept, a layer of protection in the night. More likely it was the distance between me and the pile of boxed-up what-ifs and unwanted memories lining the walls of my own bedroom. Surely this was a neutral zone, a space where panic couldn't set in. At least, that's what I thought until one Saturday night in late October, when I stared at the ceiling of his bedroom, unable to fall asleep.

I don't know exactly what triggered it. My brain seemed set on creating horrifying retellings of waking up in that car the previous winter: finding the doors locked or the back seat flooding or, spookiest of all, a stranger in the front seat, driving way over the speed limit. All I knew was that my usual symptoms were taking over: body numb, chest heavy, breathing ragged, eyes squeezed shut.

Gideon's voice felt distant, as if I was trapped underwater.

"I think," I managed to get out, "I think I'm having a panic attack."

I don't remember much else—just that Gideon grabbed a glass of water from the nightstand and held it to my lips, that he helped me count to six for my inhales and exhales, that he hugged me for what felt like hours until finally I fell asleep, the terror receding like the tide going out.

Everyone deals with shame differently. I'd become so used to packing mine away and hiding from it. But when I woke up the next morning, I felt exposed, as if I stood beneath a hot sun with no shade in sight. No one close to me had ever witnessed one of my panic attacks. I prepared myself for the worst as I shifted in bed, signaling that I was awake.

Did I? Not at all. I quickly assessed my possible escape routes.

Maybe it was the poor sleep I got the night prior, or the ear-splitting chorus of my coping mechanisms, but I did not have the energy to follow through on any of their suggestions.

I felt heat rise across my cheeks. I'd talked to many professionals over the years, but only when I had to, when something needed to be solved, when my parents weren't sure how else to help me. The specialists I'd seen varied in specialty and style, but almost all of them shared a commonality: it had not been my choice to go.

I looked at Gideon and sighed.

Even with Gideon's gentle support, it would take a month (and another debilitating panic attack) for me to begin my search for a therapist, and then another couple of weeks to find someone who had availability and accepted my health insurance.

When I arrived at my new therapist's office for our first session, I felt skeptical. If it hadn't worked before, why would it work now? And if it didn't work now, what did that mean about me?

I followed her down the hall to a room with walls painted sage green and plants lining the windowsill. We sat down across from each other, her unwavering eye contact intimidating at first.

At first, I felt the same prickly resistance I'd felt at appointments in the past, worrying that the second I shared who I *really* was, my therapist would deem me reckless or stupid or, worst of all, a lost cause.

Fortunately, my therapist was patient.

I won't sugarcoat it: It took me a long time to get to a place where I could reveal the parts of myself I'd worked so hard to box away. And even then, I wouldn't lift my eyes from my lap as I whispered my deepest insecurities and shameful moments, twisting a loose strand of fabric from my shirt around my finger until the tip turned purple.

But over time, therapy became a release. A space to let my feelings unravel. Fifty minutes of safety. And I noticed that the more I opened up, the more the Vault's chains loosened. It felt like I was ripping the wallpaper from an old house's interior, the faulty cracks beneath it finally visible.

Not unlike a remodel, change took time. I finally saw a psychia-trist, who prescribed me a low dose of an antianxiety medication that left me feeling less like a live wire. My panic attacks didn't stop, not totally. But their frequency did fall off. I stopped waiting for a cure, for a final fix. There was always something to talk about, to work through.

Of course, no path is perfect. Eight months into working with her, my therapist let me know she would no longer be accepting my insurance, that she was so sorry, that she was so honored to have been part of my journey. I fought back tears as I nodded. Finding a new therapist meant building trust with another stranger and opening up boxes I thought I'd dealt with once and for all. I felt like I was back to square one.

Later that evening, I collapsed on Gideon's couch.

It took me a beat to realize that just because I was no longer seeing my therapist didn't mean I lost everything I learned while working with her.

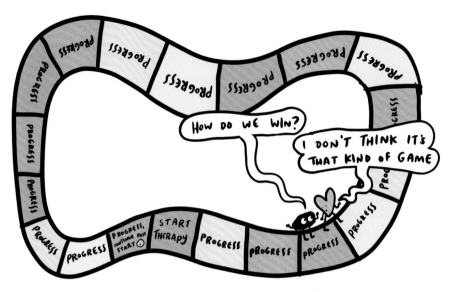

NOTE: PROGRESS MAY NOT ALWAYS FEEL LIKE PROGRESS. KEEP GOING.

I didn't know it yet, but I would find a new therapist later that year. Until then, though, I looked at the Vault, whose chains hung like an oversized T-shirt off her body after eight months of putting words to my feelings. I could keep loosening them, I thought, simply because I chose to. My therapist wasn't the only person who could listen and not recoil at who I really was.

I just had to let people in.

A SUPPORT SYSTEM CAN LOOK LIKE: FAMILY (BLOOD OR CHOSEN) · PARTNER(S) · FRIENDS · NEIGHBORS · CO-WORKERS · ONLINE COMMUNITIES · THERAPISTS · DOCTORS · KIND STRANGERS · COPING MECHANISMS (IN MODERATION) · YOURSELF ·

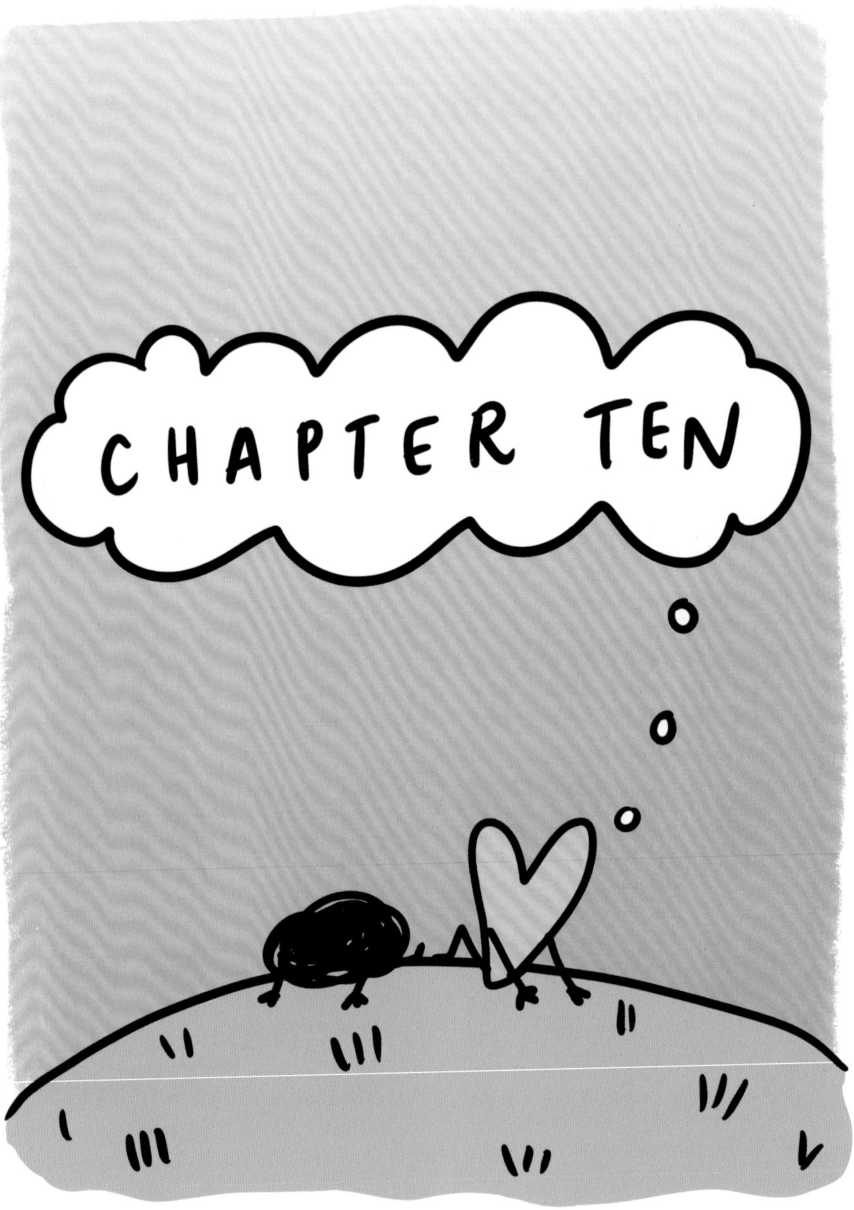
CHAPTER TEN

I really thought 2020 was going to be my year.

After all, things were going well. Weirdly well. I finally had a job I liked, a community I loved, and even on the rainiest days, Seattle had become home. But most of all, I noticed Anxiety and my coping mechanisms were getting along better than ever.

I think you can guess what happened next.

It felt like a rainstorm had swept through, the downpour washing any sense of normalcy away. I got laid off from my job. Businesses in my neighborhood closed their doors. My roommate left to stay at her parents' house and my boyfriend all but moved in, our evenings spent sitting side by side on the couch, doom-scrolling through our phones in silence.

I called my parents every day to ask what they thought would happen next, as if they could predict the unpredictable. I wavered between obsessively refreshing my Twitter feed and hiding my phone under a pillow, as if it could snuff out the notifications. I squeezed a glob of hand sanitizer into my palm after touching anything at the grocery store, as if it would act as a force field between me and the rest of the world. In fact, I felt overpowered by the "as ifs," grasping for answers that weren't even there.

But those two weeks turned into three, then four. My therapist sent me a video call link every Tuesday afternoon, each of our sessions following a similar script:

How was I feeling? It felt impossible to answer that question. Since starting therapy over a year ago, Anxiety and I had gotten better at building mutual respect (and even listening to what the other had to say). And my new therapist empowered me to distance myself from some of the coping mechanisms that weren't all too helpful.

She also introduced me to a few new friends:

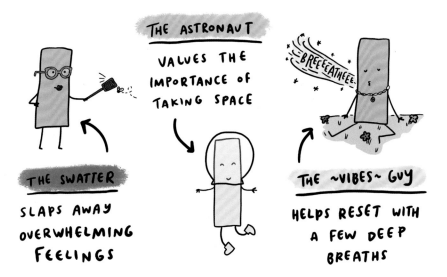

But as the global uncertainty rose with each passing day, it was hard not to fall back into old patterns.

And we weren't the only ones spiraling.

When I told my therapist it had been difficult to cope, she suggested I establish some healthy boundaries for myself.

I scheduled a mandatory team meeting later that afternoon.

It didn't take long for me to lose control of the conversation.

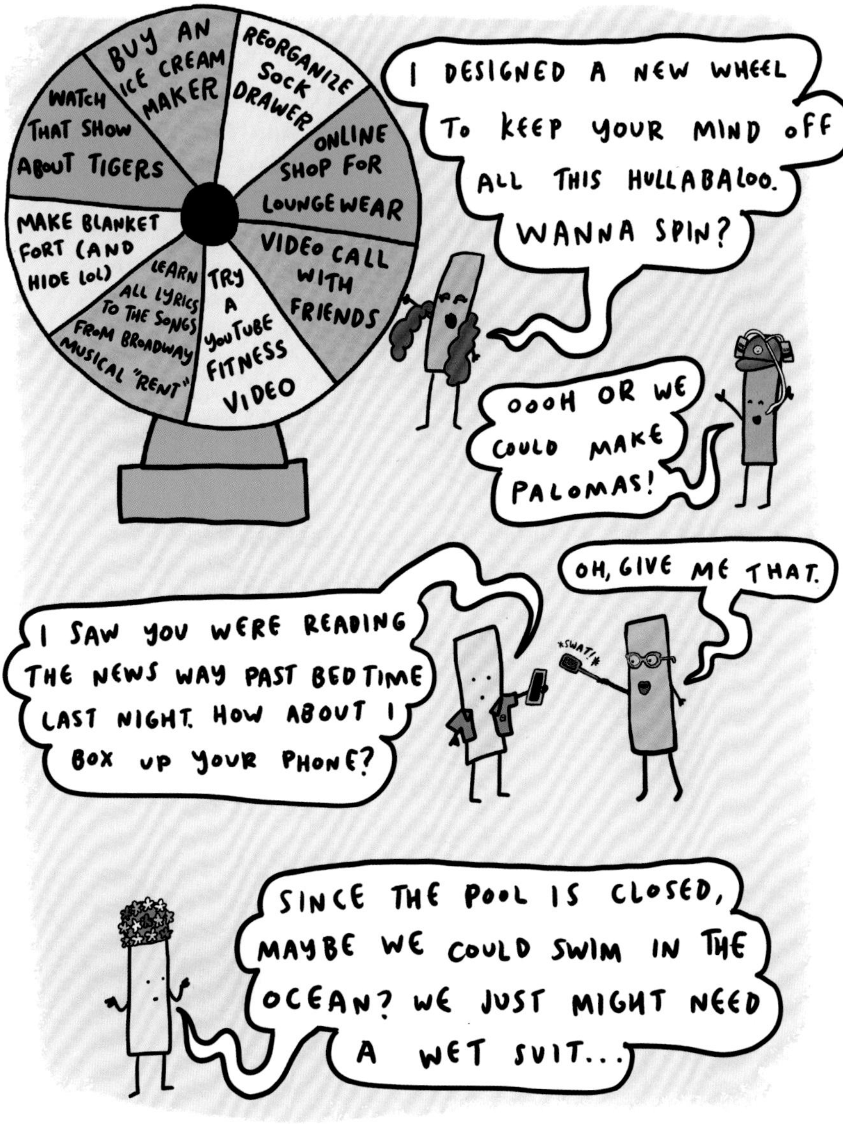
BUY AN ICE CREAM MAKER
REORGANIZE SOCK DRAWER
ONLINE SHOP FOR LOUNGEWEAR
VIDEO CALL WITH FRIENDS
TRY A YOUTUBE FITNESS VIDEO
LEARN ALL LYRICS TO THE SONGS FROM BROADWAY MUSICAL "RENT"
MAKE BLANKET FORT (AND HIDE LOL)
WATCH THAT SHOW ABOUT TIGERS
I DESIGNED A NEW WHEEL TO KEEP YOUR MIND OFF ALL THIS HULLABALOO. WANNA SPIN?
OOOH OR WE COULD MAKE PALOMAS!
I SAW YOU WERE READING THE NEWS WAY PAST BEDTIME LAST NIGHT. HOW ABOUT I BOX UP YOUR PHONE?
OH, GIVE ME THAT.
*SWAT!*
SINCE THE POOL IS CLOSED, MAYBE WE COULD SWIM IN THE OCEAN? WE JUST MIGHT NEED A WET SUIT...

But then I heard a tapping on the window.

So I grabbed my face mask and we snuck outside.

The Hiker began to walk down the street and then up another. Anxiety and I followed his lead, my legs stiff after sitting all day.

We zigzagged through my neighborhood for a while, passing houses with signs thanking health-care workers propped in the windows and chalk drawings brightening the driveways. Spring had announced itself slowly that April: the bulbs blooming from tree branches looked like popcorn, and the sky had finally traded its drab sheath of gray for a pale blue. The Hiker took none of this for granted. He tilted his head back when the sun peeked out from behind a cloud. He stopped to sniff a tulip sprouting from the earth. He smiled at dogs on walks with their owners.

After a while the breeze, cool and perfumed with sea salt, reminded me that we were getting close to the rugged coastline overlooking the Puget Sound. The Hiker seemed compelled by the scent, hastening his pace. But in my periphery, I noticed Anxiety falling behind.

We rounded the corner to the park at the edge of my neighborhood. I'd been there a few times before, but never on an evening like this.

The sky looked perfect, almost artificial, as if someone had hung up one of those cheesy sunset backdrops used for cruise ship photo-shoots or prom pictures. The sun sat just above the sound, its tanger-ine glow spilling out across the water's surface.

We weren't the only ones there. Some people sat in camping chairs while others stood, all at least six feet apart. The Hiker walked toward the chain-link fence bordering the park and leaned against the rail-ing. I followed suit, the metal cold on my forearms.

I don't know how long we stood there, eyes squinted and cheeks wind-burned pink. The sun kept sinking below the mountains, dragging dusk down like a curtain. The fabric of my mask caved in between my lips as I inhaled, and I turned my vision away from the sky to find Anxiety staring up at me.

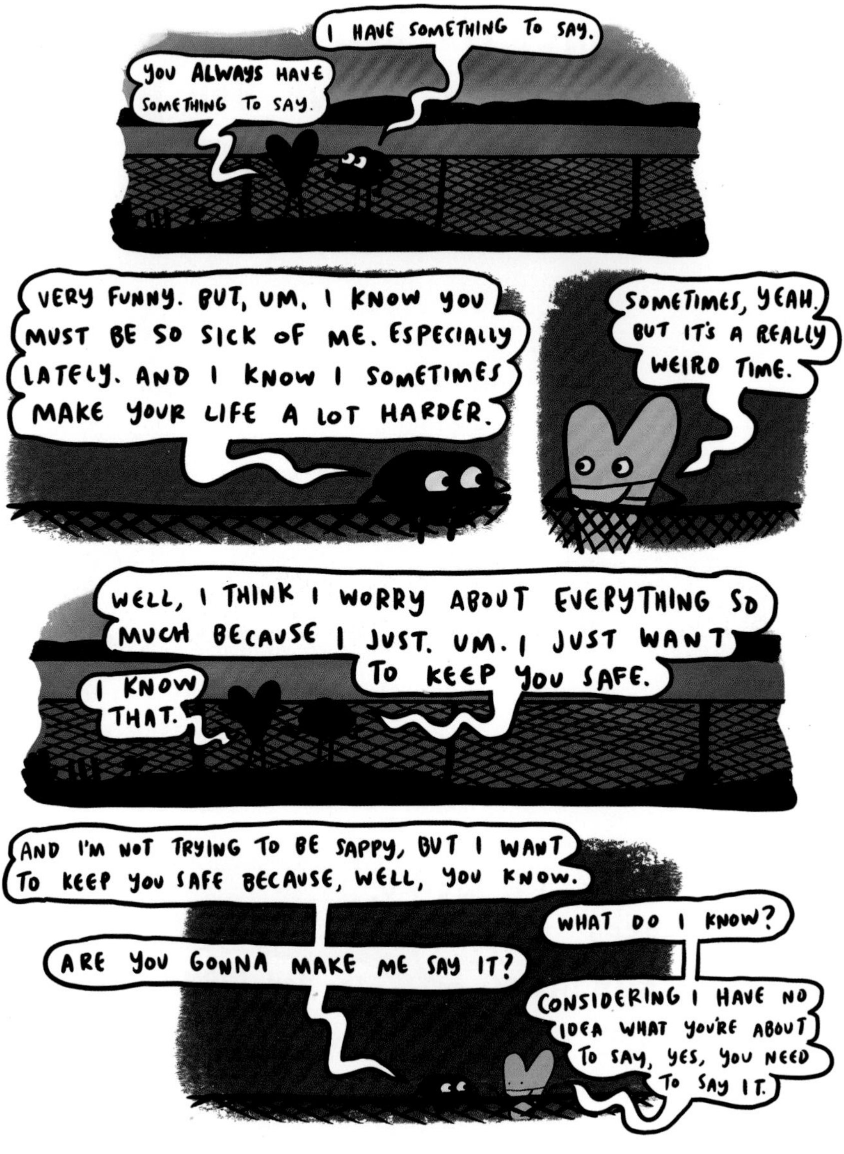

YOU ALWAYS HAVE SOMETHING TO SAY.
I HAVE SOMETHING TO SAY.
VERY FUNNY. BUT, UM. I KNOW YOU MUST BE SO SICK OF ME. ESPECIALLY LATELY. AND I KNOW I SOMETIMES MAKE YOUR LIFE A LOT HARDER.
SOMETIMES, YEAH. BUT IT'S A REALLY WEIRD TIME.
WELL, I THINK I WORRY ABOUT EVERYTHING SO MUCH BECAUSE I JUST. UM. I JUST WANT TO KEEP YOU SAFE.
I KNOW THAT.
AND I'M NOT TRYING TO BE SAPPY, BUT I WANT TO KEEP YOU SAFE BECAUSE, WELL, YOU KNOW.
WHAT DO I KNOW?
ARE YOU GONNA MAKE ME SAY IT?
CONSIDERING I HAVE NO IDEA WHAT YOU'RE ABOUT TO SAY, YES, YOU NEED TO SAY IT.

The words seemed frozen in the air between us. Love? I thought about the weight of that word and how I applied it—to my family, my friends, my partner, my dogs. To cities I'd visited, to hobbies I cherished, to certain colors and songs and book characters and ice cream flavors. I even loved parts of myself, like my creativity and my eyes and my sense of humor. But the bundle of doubt and nerves and what-ifs that seemed to fill any open space in my brain—did I love that, too?

And I meant it. I knew Anxiety's constant worrying stemmed from a deeply rooted desire to keep me secure. Alive. Okay. Better than okay, really.

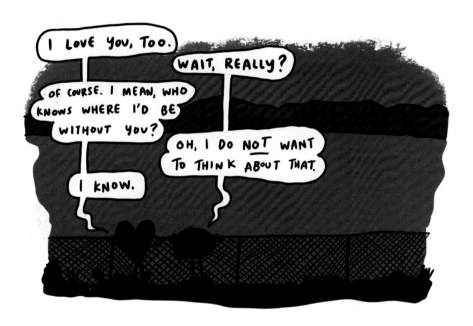

The sun had almost disappeared entirely, the only evidence of its existence an aura of hazy violet at the edge of the earth. People began to pack up their chairs and picnic blankets, ushering themselves out as the darkness moved in. A bird flew over the waves, its outline barely distinguishable from the deep blue sky behind it. But my eyes stayed trained on that last bit of daylight, a mere glimmer hanging on for just a moment longer.

Soon the sky would be a single shade of navy, studded with stars and a sliver of moon. And then it'd be something else: stark midnight, light pink dawn, wet gray afternoon. The sun would come and go. Change was constant, never-ending. I could be both scared of it and grateful for it.

And I was. At least, I would try to be. That was all I knew for sure.

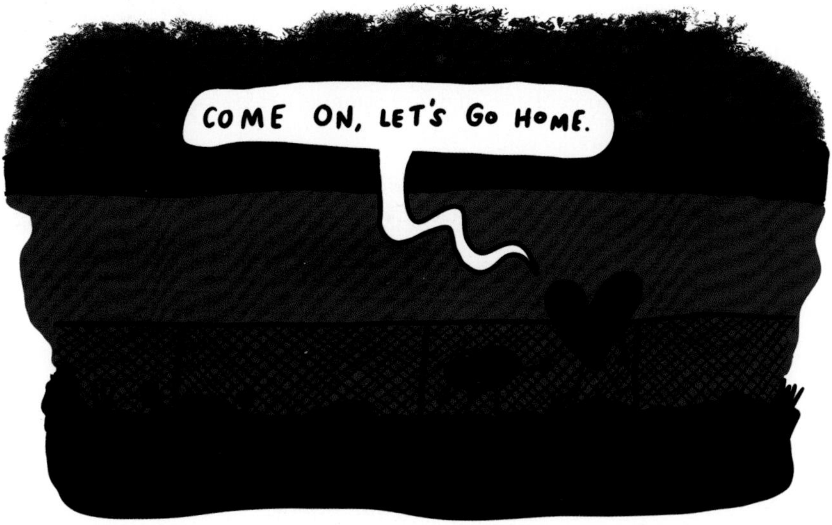
COME ON, LET'S GO HOME.

# Acknowledgments

First, a massive thanks to everyone at Neon Literary and especially my agent, Anna Sproul-Latimer. Remember when we sat on the floor of your office with burrito bowls in our laps as we tried to come up with a book title? How far we've come! Thank you for your patience through the early stages of figuring out what this book was going to be, for your guidance, and for becoming a safe space and friend. This book would not exist without you.

To my dazzling editor, Lucia Watson: from our first meeting to our correspondence throughout the writing process, you have made me feel seen in a way I never thought I would experience professionally and artistically. And, of course, a massive thanks to Suzy Swartz and the brilliant team at both Avery and Penguin Random House. Thank you for believing in this book.

I would not be the person I am today without Michelle Icard. When I met you as an insecure eleven-year-old, I thought you were the coolest adult on the planet. The fact that I now get to call you my mentor and friend would blow preteen me's mind! Thank you for answering all of my texts with enthusiasm and care, and for instilling confidence in me when I needed it most.

To my friends: you are all quite literally scattered throughout this book as little heart characters, brightening the pages just as you do my life. Thank you all for believing in me and accepting me even when my anxiety took up space. I love you all so much. I want to extend a special thank-you to Sydnee Lindblom for instilling my love of reading and writing; to Allie Gamble for encouraging me to share my art online back in 2017; to Sam Foote, Gwen Ford, and Ellie Houser for being my rocks through my tumultuous college experience (and encouraging me to write about it); to Rachel Gittelman and Petr Novodvorskiy for letting me write so much of this book from your kitchen table; to both Zakiya Brown and Priyanka Anand for the mental-health-saving walks while I was in the throes of drawing; to Carlie Stowe for reading early drafts of this book with such care; and finally, to my chickens for showing me the beauty of vulnerable, intimate friendship.

I'm profoundly grateful to the whole Dunster family for their love and support. You all feel like home to me. As for my extended family: thank you for nurturing the writer in me, even when I was a moody teen who insisted on giving out my angsty poetry as Christmas gifts.

This book is for my nana, who has read these essays more than any other person has or ever will. Thank you for being my first reader, most consistent pen pal, and number-one fan.

To Mom, the world's best cheerleader and confidant. Thank you for letting me take my own path with all its twists and turns, for picking up every late-night phone call, and for reading out loud to me even when I told you I was "too old" for that. I will never be too old to be your daughter.

To Dad, who taught me to embrace and celebrate the weird parts of myself. I feel so grateful to have such a smart, funny, and generous father. You've never questioned my goals; you've only gently suggested I reach even further.

To my sister, Charlotte, otherwise known as my original creative collaborator. I would not be half the artist or writer I am today without our marathon drawing sessions at the kitchen table (or the elaborate storylines we made up for our Beanie Babies).

To Graham, my brother and editor and dear friend all in one. Thank you for being the most trustworthy, judgment-free zone and for all the hour-long FaceTime calls that went from going over the many versions of this book to talking about everything else.

And finally, a giant heap of gratitude for my partner, Gideon, who made me tea as I stayed up late drawing and reminded me that yes, I am worthy of this project and everything else under the sun every single day. You make me feel profoundly accepted and loved.

# GLOSSARY OF COPING MECHANISMS

THE HURRICANE

THE HIDER

THE VAULT

THE DISTRACTOR

THE LIAR

THE PARTIER

THE COMPARTMENTALIZER

THE DIVER

THE WRITER

THE ~VIBES~ GUY

THE ASTRONAUT

THE SWATTER

THE HIKER